Marxism and
Literary Criticism

Marxism and Literary Criticism

TERRY EAGLETON

UNIVERSITY OF CALIFORNIA PRESS

Berkeley and Los Angeles

UNIVERSITY OF CALIFORNIA PRESS
Berkeley and Los Angeles, California

ISBN: 0-520-03243-8

Library of Congress Catalog Card Number: 76-6707

7 8 9 0

Printed in the United States of America

Contents

Preface

Marxism is a highly complex subject, and that sector of it known as Marxist literary criticism is no less so. It would therefore be impossible in this short study to do more than broach a few basic issues and raise some fundamental questions. (The book is as short as it is, incidentally, because it was originally designed for a series of brief introductory studies.) The danger with books of this kind is that they risk boring those already familiar with the subject and puzzling those for whom it is entirely new. I make little claim to originality or comprehensiveness, but I have tried at least to be neither tedious nor mystifying. I have aimed to present the topic as clearly as possible, although this, given its difficulties, is not an easy task. I hope anyway that what difficulties there may be belong to the subject rather than to the presentation.

Marxist criticism analyses literature in terms of the historical conditions which produce it; and it needs, similarly, to be aware of its own historical conditions. To give an account of a Marxist critic like, say, Georg Lukács without examining the historical factors which shape his criticism is clearly inadequate. The most valuable way of discussing Marxist criticism, then, would be an historical survey of it from Marx and Engels to the present day, charting the ways in which that criticism changes as the history in which it is rooted changes. This, however, has proved impossible for reasons of space. I have therefore chosen four central topics of Marxist criticism, and discussed various authors in the light of them; and although this means a good deal of compression and omission, it also suggests something of the coherence and continuity of the subject.

I have spoken of Marxism as a 'subject', and there is a real danger that books of this sort may contribute to precisely that kind of academicism. No doubt we shall soon see Marxist criticism comfortably wedged between Freudian and mythological approaches to literature, as yet one more stimulating academic 'approach', one more well-tilled field of inquiry for students to tramp. Before this happens, it is worth reminding ourselves of a simple fact. Marxism is a scientific theory of human societies and of the practice of transforming them; and what that means, rather more concretely, is that the narrative Marxism has to deliver is the story of the struggles of men and women to free themselves from certain forms of exploitation and oppression. There is nothing academic about those struggles, and we forget this at our cost.

The relevance to that struggle of a Marxist reading of *Paradise Lost* or *Middlemarch* is not immediately apparent. But if it is a mistake to confine Marxist criticism to the academic archives it is because it has its significant, if not central, role to play in the transformation of human societies. Marxist criticism is part of a larger body of theoretical analysis which aims to understand *ideologies* — the ideas, values and feelings by which men experience their societies at various times. And certain of those ideas, values and feelings are available to us only in literature. To understand ideologies is to understand both the past and the present more deeply; and such understanding contributes to our liberation. It is in that belief that I have written this book: a book I dedicate to the members of my class on Marxist criticism at Oxford, who have argued these issues with me to a point which makes them virtually co-authors.

1

Literature and history

Marx, Engels and criticism

If Karl Marx and Frederick Engels are better known for their political and economic rather than literary writings, this is not in the least because they regarded literature as insignificant. It is true, as Leon Trotsky remarked in *Literature and Revolution* (1924), that 'there are many people in this world who think as revolutionists and feel as philistines'; but Marx and Engels were not of this number. The writings of Karl Marx, himself the youthful author of lyric poetry, a fragment of verse-drama and an unfinished comic novel much influenced by Laurence Sterne, are laced with literary concepts and allusions; he wrote a sizeable unpublished manuscript on art and religion, and planned a journal of dramatic criticism, a full-length study of Balzac and a treatise on aesthetics. Art and literature were part of the very air Marx breathed, as a formidably cultured German intellectual in the great classical tradition of his society. His acquaintance with literature, from Sophocles to the Spanish novel, Lucretius to potboiling English fiction, was staggering in its scope; the German workers' circle he founded in Brussels devoted an evening a week to discussing the arts, and Marx himself was an inveterate theatre-goer, declaimer of poetry, devourer of every species of literary art from Augustan prose to industrial ballads. He described his own works in a letter to Engels as forming an 'artistic whole', and was scrupulously sensitive to questions of literary style, not least his own; his very first pieces of journalism argued for freedom of artistic expression. Moreover, the pressure of aesthetic concepts can be detected behind some of the most crucial categories of economic thought he employs in his mature work.[1]

Even so, Marx and Engels had rather more important tasks on their hands than the formulation of a complete aesthetic theory. Their comments on art and literature are scattered and fragmentary, glancing allusions rather than developed positions.[2] This is one reason why Marxist criticism involves more than merely re-stating cases set out by the founders of Marxism. It also involves more than what has become known in the West as the 'sociology of literature'. The sociology of literature concerns itself chiefly with what might be called the means of literary production, distribution and exchange in a particular society — how books are published, the social composition of their authors and audiences, levels of literacy, the social determinants of 'taste'. It also examines literary texts for their 'sociological' relevance, raiding literary works to abstract from them themes of interest to the social historian. There has been some excellent work in this field,[3] and it forms one aspect of Marxist criticism as a whole; but taken by itself it is neither particularly Marxist nor particularly critical. It is, indeed, for the most part a suitably tamed, degutted version of Marxist criticism, appropriate for Western consumption.

Marxist criticism is not merely a 'sociology of literature', concerned with how novels get published and whether they mention the working class. Its aim is to *explain* the literary work more fully; and this means a sensitive attention to its forms, styles and meanings.[4] But it also means grasping those forms, styles and meanings as the products of a particular history. The painter Henri Matisse once remarked that all art bears the imprint of its historical epoch, but that great art is that in which this imprint is most deeply marked. Most students of literature are taught otherwise: the greatest art is that which timelessly transcends its historical conditions. Marxist criticism has much to say on this issue, but the 'historical' analysis of literature did not of course begin with Marxism. Many thinkers before Marx had tried to account for literary works in terms of the history which produced them; and one of these, the German idealist philosopher G.W.F. Hegel, had a profound influence on Marx's own aesthetic thought. The originality of Marxist criticism, then, lies not in its historical approach to literature, but in its revolutionary understanding of history itself.

Base and superstructure

The seeds of that revolutionary understanding are planted in a famous passage in Marx and Engels's *The German Ideology* (1845-6):

The production of ideas, concepts and consciousness is first of all directly interwoven with the material intercourse of man, the language of real life. Conceiving, thinking, the spiritual intercourse of men, appear here as the direct efflux of men's material behaviour ... we do not proceed from what men say, imagine, conceive, nor from men as described, thought of, imagined, conceived, in order to arrive at corporeal man; rather we proceed from the really active man ... Consciousness does not determine life: life determines consciousness.

A fuller statement of what this means can be found in the Preface to *A Contribution to the Critique of Political Economy* (1859):

In the social production of their life, men enter into definite relations that are indispensable and independent of their will, *relations of production* which correspond to a definite stage of development of their material productive *forces*. The sum total of these relations of production constitutes the economic structure of society, the real foundation, on which rises a legal and political superstructure and to which correspond definite forms of social consciousness. The mode of production of material life conditions the social, political and intellectual life process in general. It is not the consciousness of men that determines their being, but on the contrary, their social being that determines their consciousness.

The social relations between men, in other words, are bound up with the way they produce their material life. Certain 'productive forces' — say, the organisation of labour in the middle ages — involve the social relations of villein to lord we know as feudalism. At a later stage, the development of new modes of productive organisation is based on a changed set of social relations — this time between the capitalist class who owns those means of production, and the proletarian class whose labour-power the capitalist buys for profit. Taken together, these 'forces' and 'relations' of production form what Marx calls 'the economic structure of society', or what is more commonly known by Marxism as the economic 'base' or 'infrastructure'. From this economic base, in every period, emerges a 'superstructure' — certain forms of law and politics, a certain kind of state, whose essential function is to legitimate the power of the social class which owns the means of economic production. But the superstructure contains more than this: it also consists of certain 'definite forms of social consciousness' (political, religious, ethical, aesthetic and so on), which is what Marxism designates as *ideology*. The function of ideology, also, is to legitimate the power of the ruling class in society; in the last analysis, the dominant ideas of a society are the ideas of its ruling class.[6]

Art, then, is for Marxism part of the 'superstructure' of society. It is (with qualifications we shall make later) part of a society's ideology — an element in that complex structure of social perception which ensures that the situation in which one social class has power over the others is either seen by most members of the society as 'natural', or not seen at all. To understand literature, then, means understanding the total social process of which it is part. As the Russian Marxist critic Georgy Plekhanov put it: 'The social mentality of an age is conditioned by that age's social relations. This is nowhere quite as evident as in the history of art and literature'.[7] Literary works are not mysteriously inspired, or explicable simply in terms of their authors' psychology. They are forms of perception, particular ways of seeing the world; and as such they have a relation to that dominant way of seeing the world which is the 'social mentality' or ideology of an age. That ideology, in turn, is the product of the concrete social relations into which men enter at a particular time and place; it is the way those class-relations are experienced, legitimized and perpetuated. Moreover, men are not free to choose their social relations; they are constrained into them by material necessity — by the nature and stage of development of their mode of economic production.

To understand *King Lear*, *The Dunciad* or *Ulysses* is therefore to do more than interpret their symbolism, study their literary history and add footnotes about sociological facts which enter into them. It is first of all to understand the complex, indirect relations between those works and the ideological worlds they inhabit — relations which emerge not just in 'themes' and 'preoccupations', but in style, rhythm, image, quality and (as we shall see later) *form*. But we do not understand ideology either unless we grasp the part it plays in the society as a whole — how it consists of a definite, historically relative structure of perception which underpins the power of a particular social class. This is not an easy task, since an ideology is never a simple reflection of a ruling class's ideas; on the contrary, it is always a complex phenomenon, which may incorporate conflicting, even contradictory, views of the world. To understand an ideology, we must analyse the precise relations between different classes in a society; and to do that means grasping where those classes stand in relation to the mode of production.

All this may seem a tall order to the student of literature who thought he was merely required to discuss plot and characterization. It may seem a confusion of literary criticism with disciplines like politics and economics which ought to be kept separate. But it is, nonetheless, essential for the fullest explanation of any work of literature. Take, for example, the great Placido Gulf scene in Conrad's *Nostromo*. To evaluate the fine artistic force of this episode, as Decoud and Nostromo are isolated in utter darkness on the slowly sinking lighter, involves us in subtly placing the scene within the imaginative vision of the novel as a whole. The radical pessimism of that vision (and to grasp it fully we must, of course, relate *Nostromo* to the rest of Conrad's fiction) cannot simply be accounted for in terms of 'psychological' factors in Conrad himself; for individual psychology is also a *social* product. The pessimism of Conrad's world view is rather a unique transformation into art of an ideological pessimism rife in his period — a sense of history as futile and cyclical, of individuals as impenetrable and solitary, of human values as relativistic and irrational, which marks a drastic crisis in the ideology of the Western bourgeois class to which Conrad allied himself. There were good reasons for that ideological crisis, in the history of imperialist capitalism throughout this period. Conrad did not, of course, merely anonymously reflect that history in his fiction; every writer is individually placed in society, responding to a general history from his own particular standpoint, making sense of it in his own concrete terms. But it is not difficult to see how Conrad's personal standing, as an 'aristocratic' Polish exile deeply committed to English conservatism, intensified for him the crisis of English bourgeois ideology.[8]

It is also possible to see in these terms why that scene in the Placido Gulf should be artistically fine. To write well is more than a matter of 'style'; it also means having at one's disposal an ideological perspective which can penetrate to the realities of men's experience in a certain situation. This is certainly what the Placido Gulf scene does; and it can do it, not just because its author happens to have an excellent prose-style, but because his historical situation allows him access to such insights. Whether those insights are in political terms 'progressive' or 'reactionary' (Conrad's are certainly the latter) is not the point — any more than it is to the point that most of the agreed major writers of the twentieth century — Yeats, Eliot, Pound, Lawrence — are political conservatives who each had truck with fascism. Marxist criticism, rather than apologising for that fact, explains it — sees that, in the absence of genuinely revolutionary art, only a radical conservatism, hostile like Marxism to the withered values of liberal bourgeois society, could produce the most significant literature.

Literature and superstructure

It would be a mistake to imply that Marxist criticism moves mechanically from 'text' to 'ideology' to 'social relations' to 'productive forces'. It is concerned, rather, with the *unity* of these 'levels' of society. Literature may be part of the superstructure, but it is not merely the passive reflection of the economic base. Engels makes this clear, in a letter to Joseph Bloch in 1890:

> According to the materialist conception of history, the determining element in history is *ultimately* the production and reproduction in real life. More than this neither Marx nor I have ever asserted. If therefore somebody twists this into the statement that the economic element is the *only* determining one, he transforms it into a meaningless, abstract and absurd phrase. The economic situation is the basis, but the various elements of the superstructure — political forms of the class struggle and its consequences, constitutions established by the victorious class after a successful battle, etc. — forms of law — and then even the reflexes of all these actual struggles in the brains of the combatants: political, legal, and philosophical theories, religious ideas and their further development into systems of dogma — also exercise their influence upon the course of the historical struggles and in many cases preponderate in determining their *form*.

Engels wants to deny that there is any mechanical, one-to-one correspondence between base and superstructure; elements of the superstructure constantly react back upon and influence the economic base. The materialist theory of history denies that art can *in itself* change the course of history; but it insists that art can be an active element in such change. Indeed, when Marx came to consider the relation between base and super-structure, it was art which he selected as an instance of the complexity and indirectness of that relationship:

> In the case of the arts, it is well known that certain periods of their flowering are out of all proportion to the general development of society, hence also to the material foundation, the skeletal structure, as it were, of its organisation. For example, the Greeks compared to the moderns or also Shakespeare. It is even recognised that certain forms of art, e.g. the epic, can no longer be pro-duced in their world epoch-making, classical stature as soon as the production of art, as such, begins; that is, that certain significant forms within the realm of the arts are possible only at an undeveloped stage of artistic development. If this is the case with the relation between different kinds of art within the realm of art, it is already less puzzling that it is the case in the relation of the entire realm to the general development of society. The difficulty consists only in the general formulation of these contradictions. As soon as they have been specified, they are already clarified.[9]

Marx is considering here what he calls 'the unequal relationship of the development of material production...to artistic production'. It does not follow that the greatest artistic achievements depend upon the highest development of the productive forces, as the example of the Greeks, who produced major art in an economically undeveloped society, clearly evidences. Certain major artistic forms like the epic are only *possible* in an undeveloped society. Why then, Marx goes on to ask, do we still respond to such forms, given our historical distance from them?:

> But the difficulty lies not in understanding that the Greek arts and epic are bound up with certain forms of social development. The difficulty is that they still afford us artistic pleasure and that in a certain respect they count as a norm and as an unattainable model.

Why does Greek art still give us aesthetic pleasure? The answer which Marx goes on to provide has been universally lambasted by unsympathetic commentators as lamely inept:

> A man cannot become a child again, or he becomes childish. But does he not find joy in the child's naiveté, and must he himself not strive to reproduce its truth at a higher stage? Does not the true character of each epoch come alive in the nature of its children? Why should not the historic childhood of humanity, its most beautiful unfolding, as a stage never to return, exercise an eternal charm? There are unruly children and precocious children. Many of the old peoples belong in this category. The Greeks were normal children. The charm of their art for us is not in contradiction to the undeveloped stage of society on which it grew. (It) is its result, rather, and is inextricably bound up, rather, with the fact that

the unripe social conditions under which it arose, and could alone rise, can never return.

So our liking for Greek art is a nostalgic lapse back into childhood — a piece of unmaterialist sentimentalism which hostile critics have gladly pounced on. But the passage can only be treated thus if it is rudely ripped from the context to which it belongs — the draft manuscripts of 1857, known today as the *Grundrisse*. Once returned to that context, the meaning becomes instantly apparent. The Greeks, Marx is arguing, were able to produce major art not *in spite of* but *because of* the undeveloped state of their society. In ancient societies, which have not yet undergone the fragmenting 'division of labour' known to capitalism, the overwhelming of 'quality' by 'quantity' which results from commodity-production and the restless, continual development of the productive forces, a certain 'measure' or harmony can be achieved between man and Nature — a harmony precisely dependent upon the *limited* nature of Greek society. The 'childlike' world of the Greeks is attractive because it thrives within certain measured limits — measures and limits which are brutally overridden by bourgeois society in its limitless demand to produce and consume. Historically, it is essential that this constricted society should be broken up as the productive forces expand beyond its frontiers; but when Marx speaks of 'striv(ing) to reproduce its truth at a higher stage', he is clearly speaking of the communist society of the future, where unlimited resources will serve an unlimitedly developing man.[10]

Two questions, then, emerge from Marx's

formulations in the *Grundrisse*. The first concerns the relation between 'base' and 'superstructure'; the second concerns our own relation in the present with past art. To take the second question first: how can it be that we moderns still find aesthetic appeal in the cultural products of past, vastly different societies? In a sense, the answer Marx gives is no different from the answer to the question: How is it that we moderns still respond to the exploits of, say, Spartacus? We respond to Spartacus or Greek sculpture because our own history links us to those ancient societies; we find in them an undeveloped phase of the forces which condition us. Moreover, we find in those ancient societies a primitive image of 'measure' between man and Nature which capitalist society necessarily destroys, and which socialist society can reproduce at an incomparably higher level. We ought, in other words, to think of 'history' in wider terms than our own contemporary history. To ask how Dickens relates to history is not just to ask how he relates to Victorian England, for that society was itself the product of a long history which includes men like Shakespeare and Milton. It is a curiously narrowed view of history which defines it merely as the 'contemporary moment' and relegates all else to the 'universal'. One answer to the problem of past and present is suggested by Bertolt Brecht, who argues that 'we need to develop the historical sense...into a real sensual delight. When our theatres perform plays of other periods they like to annihilate distance, fill in the gap, gloss over the differences. But what comes then of our delight in comparisons, in distance, in dissimilarity — which is at the same time a delight in what is close and proper to ourselves?'[11]

The other problem posed by the *Grundrisse* is the relation between base and superstructure. Marx is clear that these two aspects of society do not form a *symmetrical* relationship, dancing a harmonious minuet hand-in-hand throughout history. Each element of a society's superstructure — art, law, politics, religion — has its own tempo of development, its own internal evolution, which is not reducible to a mere expression of the class struggle or the state of the economy. Art, as Trotsky comments, has 'a very high degree of autonomy'; it is not tied in any simple one-to-one way to the mode of production. And yet Marxism claims too that, in the last analysis, art is determined by that mode of production. How are we to explain this apparent discrepancy?

Let us take a concrete literary example. A 'vulgar Marxist' case about T.S. Eliot's *The Waste Land* might be that the poem is directly determined by ideological and economic factors — by the spiritual emptiness and exhaustion of bourgeois ideology which springs from that crisis of imperialist capitalism known as the First World War. This is to explain the poem as an immediate 'reflection' of those conditions; but it clearly fails to take into account a whole series of 'levels' which 'mediate' between the text itself and capitalist economy. It says nothing, for instance, about the social situation of Eliot himself — a writer living an ambiguous relationship with English society, as an 'aristocratic' American expatriate who became a glorified City clerk and yet identified deeply with the conservative-traditionalist, rather than bourgeois-commercialist, elements of English ideology. It says nothing about that ideology's more general forms — nothing of its structure, content, internal complexity, and how all these are produced by the extremely complex class-relations of English society at the time. It is silent about the form and language of *The Waste Land* — about why Eliot, despite his extreme political conservatism, was an *avant-garde* poet who selected certain 'progressive' experimental techniques from the history of literary forms available to him, and on what ideological basis he did this. We learn nothing from this approach about the social conditions which gave rise at the time to certain forms of 'spirituality', part-Christian, part-Buddhist, which the poem draws on; or of what role a certain kind of bourgeois anthropology (Fraser) and bourgeois philosophy (F.H. Bradley's idealism) used by the poem fulfilled in the ideological formation of the period. We are unilluminated about Eliot's social position as an artist, part of a self-consciously erudite, experimental élite with particular modes of publication (the small press, the little magazine) at their disposal; or about the kind of audience which that implied, and its effect on the poem's styles and devices. We remain ignorant about the relation between the poem and the aesthetic theories associated with it — of what role that aesthetic plays in the ideology of the time, and how it shapes the construction of the poem itself.

Any complete understanding of *The Waste Land* would need to take these (and other) factors into account. It is not a matter of *reducing* the poem to the state of contemporary capitalism; but neither is it a matter of introducing so many judicious complications that anything as crude as capitalism may to all intents and purposes be forgotten. On the contrary: all of the elements I have enumerated (the author's class-position, ideological forms and their relation to literary forms, 'spirituality' and philosophy, techniques of literary production, aesthetic theory) are directly relevant to the base/superstructure model. What Marxist criticism looks for is the unique *conjuncture* of these elements which we know as *The Waste Land*.[12] No one of these elements can be conflated with another: each has its own relative independence. *The Waste Land* can indeed be explained as a poem which springs from a crisis of bourgeois ideology, but it has no simple correspondence with that crisis or with the political and economic conditions which produced it. (As a poem, it does not of course *know itself* as a product of a particular ideological crisis, for if it did it would cease to exist. It needs to translate that crisis into 'universal' terms — to grasp it as part of an unchanging human condition, shared alike by ancient Egyptians and modern man.) *The Waste Land's* relation to the real history of its time, then, is highly *mediated;* and in this it is like all works of art.

Literature and ideology

Frederick Engels remarks in *Ludwig Feuerbach and the End of Classical German Philosophy* (1888) that art is far richer and more 'opaque' than political and economic theory because it is less purely ideological. It is important here to grasp the precise meaning for Marxism of 'ideology'. Ideology is not in the first place a set of doctrines; it signifies the way men live out their roles in class-society, the values, ideas and images which tie them to their social functions and so prevent them from a true knowledge of society as a whole. In this sense *The Waste Land* is ideological: it shows a man making sense of his experience in ways that prohibit a true understanding of his society, ways that are consequently false. All art springs from an ideological conception of the world; there is no such thing, Plekhanov comments, as a work of art entirely devoid of ideological content. But Engels' remark suggests that art has a more complex relationship to ideology than law and political theory, which rather more transparently embody the interests of a ruling class. The question, then, is what relationship art has to ideology.

This is not an easy question to answer. Two extreme, opposite positions are possible here. One is that literature is *nothing but* ideology in a certain artistic form — that works of literature are just expressions of the ideologies of their time. They are prisoners of 'false consciousness', unable to reach beyond it to arrive at the truth. It is a position characteristic of much 'vulgar Marxist' criticism, which tends to see literary works merely as reflections of dominant ideologies. As such, it is unable to explain, for one thing, why so much literature actually *challenges* the ideological assumptions of its time. The opposite case seizes on the fact that so much literature challenges the ideology it confronts, and makes this part of the definition of literary art itself. Authentic art, as Ernst Fischer argues in his significantly entitled *Art Against Ideology* (1969), always transcends the ideological limits of its time, yielding us insight into the realities which ideology hides from view.

Both of these cases seem to me too simple. A more subtle (although still incomplete) account of the relationship between literature and ideology is provided by the French Marxist theorist Louis Althusser.[13] Althusser argues that art cannot be reduced to ideology: it has, rather, a particular *relationship* to it. Ideology signifies the imaginary ways in which men experience the real world, which is, of course, the kind of experience literature gives us too — what it feels like to live in particular conditions, rather than a conceptual analysis of those conditions. However, art does more than just passively reflect that experience. It is held within ideology, but also manages to distance itself from it, to the point where it permits us to 'feel' and 'perceive' the ideology from which it springs. In doing this, art does not enable us to *know* the truth which ideology conceals, since for Althusser 'knowledge' in the strict sense means *scientific* knowledge — the kind of knowledge of, say, capitalism which Marx's *Capital* rather than Dickens's *Hard Times* allows us. The difference between science and art is not that they deal with different objects, but that they deal with the same objects in different ways. Science gives us conceptual knowledge of a situation; art gives us the experience of that situation, which is equivalent to ideology. But by doing this, it allows us to 'see' the nature of that ideology, and thus begins to move us towards that full understanding of ideology which is scientific knowledge.

How literature can do this is more fully developed by one of Althusser's colleagues, Pierre Macherey.

In his *Pour Une Théorie de la Production Littéraire* (1966), Macherey distinguishes between what he terms 'illusion' (meaning, essentially, ideology), and 'fiction'. Illusion — the ordinary ideological experience of men — is the material on which the writer goes to work; but in working on it he transforms it into something different, lends it a shape and structure. It is by giving ideology a determinate form, fixing it within certain fictional limits, that art is able to distance itself from it, thus revealing to us the limits of that ideology. In doing this, Macherey claims, art contributes to our deliverance from the ideological illusion.

I find the comments of both Althusser and Macherey at crucial points ambiguous and obscure; but the relation they propose between literature and ideology is nonetheless deeply suggestive. Ideology, for both critics, is more than an amorphous body of free-floating images and ideas; in any society it has a certain structural coherence. Because it possesses such relative coherence, it can be the object of scientific analysis; and since literary texts 'belong' to ideology, they too can be the object of such scientific analysis. A scientific criticism would seek to explain the literary work in terms of the ideological structure of which it is part, yet which it transforms in its art: it would search out the principle which both ties the work to ideology and distances it from it. The finest Marxist criticism has indeed done precisely that; Macherey's starting-point is Lenin's brilliant analyses of Tolstoy.[14] To do this, however, means grasping the literary work as a *formal* structure; and it is to this question that we can now turn.

Form and
content

History and form

In his early essay *The Evolution of Modern Drama*
(1909), the Hungarian Marxist critic Georg Lukács
writes that 'the truly social element in literature is
the form'. This is not the kind of comment which
has come to be expected of Marxist criticism. For
one thing, Marxist criticism has traditionally
opposed all kinds of literary formalism, attacking
that inbred attention to sheerly technical properties
which robs literature of historical significance and
reduces it to an aesthetic game. It has, indeed, noted
the relationship between such critical technocracy
and the behaviour of advanced capitalist
societies.[1] For another thing, a good deal of
Marxist criticism has in practice paid scant
attention to questions of artistic form, shelving the
issue in its dogged pursuit of political content. Marx
himself believed that literature should reveal a unity
of form and content, and burnt some of his own
early lyric poems on the grounds that their
rhapsodic feelings were dangerously unrestrained;

but he was also suspicious of excessively formalistic writing. In an early newspaper article on Silesian weavers' songs, he claimed that mere stylistic exercises led to 'perverted content', which in turn impresses the stamp of 'vulgarity' on literary form. He shows, in other words, a *dialectical* grasp of the relations in question: form is the product of content, but reacts back upon it in a double-edged relationship. Marx's early comment about oppressively formalistic law in the *Rheinische Zeitung* — 'form is of no value unless it is the form of its content' — could equally be applied to his aesthetic views.

In arguing for a unity of form and content, Marx was being faithful to the Hegelian tradition he inherited. Hegel had argued in the *Philosophy of Fine Art* (1835) that 'every definite content determines a form suitable to it'. 'Defectiveness of form', he maintained, 'arises from defectiveness of content'. Indeed for Hegel the history of art can be written in terms of the varying relations between form and content. Art manifests different stages in the development of what Hegel calls the 'World-Spirit', the 'Idea' or the 'Absolute'; this is the 'content' of art, which successively strives to embody itself adequately in artistic form. At an early stage of historical development, the World-Spirit can find no adequate formal realization: ancient sculpture, for example, reveals how the 'Spirit' is obstructed and overwhelmed by an excess of sensual material which it is unable to mould to its own purposes. Greek classical art, on the other hand, achieves an harmonious unity between content and form, the spiritual and the material: here, for a brief historical moment, 'content' finds its entirely appropriate embodiment. In the modern world, however, and most typically in Romanticism, the spiritual absorbs the sensual, content overwhelms form. Material forms give way before the highest development of the Spirit, which like Marx's productive forces have outstripped the limited classical moulds which previously contained them.

It would be mistaken to think that Marx adopted Hegel's aesthetic wholesale. Hegel's aesthetic is idealist, drastically oversimplifying and only to a limited extent dialectical; and in any case Marx disagreed with Hegel over several concrete aesthetic issues. But both thinkers share the belief that artistic form is no mere quirk on the part of the individual artist. Forms are historically determined by the kind of 'content' they have to embody; they are changed, transformed, broken down and revolutionized as that content itself changes. 'Content' is in this sense prior to 'form', just as for Marxism it is changes in a society's material 'content', its mode of production, which determine the 'forms' of its superstructure. 'Form itself', Fredric Jameson has remarked in his *Marxism and Form* (1971), 'is but the working out of content in the realm of the superstructure'. To those who reply irritably that form and content are inseparable anyway — that the distinction is artificial — it is as well to say immediately that this is of course true *in practice*. Hegel himself recognized this: 'Content', he wrote, 'is nothing but the transformation of form into content, and form is nothing but the transformation of content into form'. But if form and content are inseparable in practice, they are theoretically distinct. This is why we can talk of the varying *relations* between the two.

Those relations, however, are not easy to grasp. Marxist criticism sees form and content as dialectically related, and yet wants to assert in the end the primacy of content in determining form.[2] The point is put, tortuously but correctly, by Ralph Fox in his *The Novel and the People* (1937), when he declares that 'Form is produced by content, is identical and one with it, and, though the primacy is on the side of content, form reacts on content and never remains passive.' This dialectical conception of the form-content relationship sets itself against two opposed positions. On the one hand, it attacks that formalist school (epitomized by the Russian Formalists of the 1920s) for whom content is merely a function of form — for whom the content of a poem is selected merely to reinforce the technical devices the poem deploys.[3] But it also criticizes the 'vulgar Marxist' notion that artistic form is merely an artifice, externally imposed on the turbulent content of history itself. Such a position is to be found in Christopher Caudwell's *Studies in a Dying Culture* (1938). In that book, Caudwell distinguishes between what he calls 'social being' — the vital, instinctual stuff of human experience — and a society's forms of consciousness. Revolution occurs when those forms, having become ossified and obsolete, are burst asunder by the dynamic, chaotic flood of 'social being' itself. Caudwell, in other words, thinks of 'social being' (*content*) as inherently formless, and of forms as inherently restrictive; he lacks, that is to say, a sufficiently dialectical understanding of the relations at issue. What he does not see is that 'form' does not merely process ✓

the raw material of 'content', because that content (whether social or literary) is for Marxism already *informed*; it has a significant structure. Caudwell's view is merely a variant of the bourgeois critical commonplace that art 'organizes the chaos of reality'. (What is the ideological significance of seeing reality as chaotic?) Fredric Jameson, by contrast, speaks of the 'inner logic of content', of which social or literary forms are transformative products.

Given such a limited view of the form-content relationship, it is not surprising that English Marxist critics of the 1930s fall often enough into the 'vulgar Marxist' mistake of raiding literary works for their ideological content and relating this directly to the class-struggle or the economy.[4] It is against this danger that Lukács's comment is meant to warn: the true bearers of ideology in art are the very forms, rather than abstractable content, of the work itself. We find the impress of history in the literary work precisely *as literary*, not as some superior form of social documentation.

Form and ideology

What does it mean to say that literary form is ideological? In a suggestive comment in *Literature and Revolution*, Leon Trotsky maintains that 'The relationship between form and content is determined by the fact that the new form is discovered, proclaimed and evolved under the pressure of an inner need, of a collective psychological demand which, like everything else...has its social roots.' Significant developments in literary form, then, result from significant changes in ideology. They embody new ways of perceiving social reality and (as we shall see later) new relations between artist and audience. This is evident enough if we look at well-charted examples like the rise of the novel in eighteenth-century England. The novel, as Ian Watt has argued,[5] reveals in its very *form* a changed set of ideological interests. No matter what content a particular novel of the time may have, it shares certain formal structures with other such works: a shifting of interest from the romantic and supernatural to individual psychology and 'routine' experience; a concept of life-like, substantial 'character'; a concern with the material fortunes of an individual protagonist who moves through an unpredictably evolving, linear narrative and so on. This changed form, Watt claims, is the product of an increasingly confident bourgeois class, whose consciousness has broken beyond the limits of older, 'aristocratic' literary conventions. Plekhanov argues rather similarly in *French Dramatic Literature and French 18th Century Painting*[6] that the transition from classical tragedy to sentimental comedy in France reflects a shift from aristocratic to bourgeois values. Or take the break from 'naturalism' to 'expressionism' in the European theatre around the turn of the century. This, as Raymond Williams has suggested,[7] signals a breakdown in certain dramatic conventions which in turn embody specific 'structures of feeling', a set of received ways of perceiving and responding to reality. Expressionism feels the need to transcend the limits of a naturalistic theatre which assumes the ordinary bourgeois world to be solid, to rip open that

deception and dissolve its social relations, penetrating by symbol and fantasy to the estranged,
self-divided psyches which 'normality' conceals. The
transforming of a stage convention, then, signifies a
deeper transformation in bourgeois ideology, as
confident mid-Victorian notions of selfhood and
relationship began to splinter and crumble in the
face of growing world capitalist crises.

There is, needless to say, no simple, symmetrical
relationship between changes in literary form and
changes in ideology. Literary form, as Trotsky
reminds us, has a high degree of autonomy; it
evolves partly in accordance with its own internal
pressures, and does not merely bend to every
ideological wind that blows. Just as for Marxist
economic theory each economic formation tends to
contain traces of older, superseded modes of
production, so traces of older literary forms survive
within new ones. Form, I would suggest, is always a
complex unity of at least three elements: it is partly
shaped by a 'relatively autonomous' literary history
of forms; it crystallizes out of certain dominant
ideological structures, as we have seen in the case of
the novel; and as we shall see later, it embodies
a specific set of relations between author and
audience. It is the dialectical unity between these
elements that Marxist criticism is concerned to
analyse. In selecting a form, then, the writer finds his
choice already ideologically circumscribed. He may
combine and transmute forms available to him from
a literary tradition, but these forms themselves, as
well as his permutation of them, are ideologically
significant. The languages and devices a writer finds
to hand are already saturated with certain

ideological modes of perception, certain codified ways of interpreting reality;[8] and the extent to which he can modify or remake those languages depends on more than his personal genius. It depends on whether at that point in history, 'ideology' is such that they must and can be changed.

Lukács and literary form

It is in the work of Georg Lukács that the problem of literary form has been most thoroughly explored.[9] In his early, pre-Marxist work, *The Theory of the Novel* (1920), Lukács follows Hegel in seeing the novel as the 'bourgeois epic', but an epic which unlike its classical counterpart reveals the homelessness and alienation of man in modern society. In Greek classical society man is at home in the universe, moving within a rounded, complete world of immanent meaning which is adequate to his soul's demands. The novel arises when that harmonious integration of man and his world is shattered; the hero of fiction is now in search of a totality, estranged from a world either too large or too narrow to give shape to his desires. Haunted by the disparity between empirical reality and a vanished absolute, the novel's form is typically *ironic*; it is 'the epic of a world abandoned by God'.

Lukács rejected this cosmic pessimism when he became a Marxist; but much of his later work on the novel retains the Hegelian emphases of *The Theory of the Novel*. For the Marxist Lukács of *Studies in European Realism* and *The Historical Novel*, the greatest artists are those who can recapture and recreate a harmonious totality of human life. In a society where the general and the particular, the conceptual and the sensuous, the social and the individual are increasingly torn apart by the 'alienations' of capitalism, the great writer draws these dialectically together into a complex totality. His fiction thus mirrors, in microcosmic form, the complex totality of society itself. In doing this, great art combats the alienation and fragmentation of capitalist society, projecting a rich, many-sided image of human wholeness. Lukács names such art 'realism', and takes it to include the Greeks and Shakespeare as much as Balzac and Tolstoy; the three great periods of historical 'realism' are ancient Greece, the Renaissance, and France in the early nineteenth century. A 'realist' work is rich in a complex, comprehensive set of relations between man, nature and history; and these relations embody and unfold what for Marxism is most 'typical' about a particular phase of history. By the 'typical' Lukács denotes those latent forces in any society which are from a Marxist viewpoint most historically significant and progressive, which lay bare the society's inner structure and dynamic. The task of the realist writer is to flesh out these 'typical' trends and forces in sensuously realized individuals and actions; in doing so he links the individual to the social whole, and informs each concrete particular of social life with the power of the 'world-historical' — the significant movements of history itself.

Lukács's major critical concepts — 'totality', 'typicality', 'world-historical' — are essentially Hegelian rather than directly Marxist, although Marx and Engels certainly use the notion of 'typicality' in their own literary criticism. Engels remarked in a letter to Lassalle that true character must combine typicality with individuality; and both he and Marx thought this a major achievement of Shakespeare and Balzac. A 'typical' or 'representative' character incarnates historical forces without thereby ceasing to be richly individualized; and for a writer to dramatize those historical forces he must, for Lukács, be 'progressive' in his art. All great art is socially progressive in the sense that, whatever the author's conscious political allegiance (and in the case of Scott and Balzac it is overtly reactionary), it realizes the vital 'world-historical' forces of an epoch which make for change and growth, revealing their unfolding potential in its fullest complexity. The realist writer, then, penetrates through the accidental phenomena of social life to disclose the essences or essentials of a condition, selecting and combining them into a total form and fleshing them out in concrete experience.

Whether or not a writer can do this depends for Lukács not just on his personal skill but on his position within history. The great realist writers arise from a history which is visibly in the making; the historical novel, for example, appears as a *genre* at a point of revolutionary turbulence in the early nineteenth century, where it was possible for writers to grasp their own present as *history* — or, to put it in Lukács's phrase, to see past history as 'the pre-history of the present'. Shakespeare, Scott, Balzac and Tolstoy can produce major realist art because they are present at the tumultuous birth of an historical epoch, and so are dramatically engaged with the vividly exposed 'typical' conflicts and dynamics of their societies. It is this historical 'content' which lays the basis for their formal achievement; 'richness and profundity of created characters', Lukács claims, 'relies upon the richness and profundity of the total social process'.[10] For the successors of the realists — for, say, Flaubert who follows Balzac — history is already an inert object, an externally given fact no longer imaginable as men's dynamic product. Realism, deprived of the historical conditions which gave it birth, splinters and declines into 'naturalism' on the one hand and 'formalism' on the other.

The crucial transition here for Lukács is the failure of the European revolutions of 1848 — a failure which signals the defeat of the proletariat, seals the demise of the progressive, heroic period of bourgeois power, freezes the class-struggle and cues the bourgeoisie for its proper, sordidly unheroic task of consolidating capitalism. Bourgeois ideology forgets its previous revolutionary ideals, de-historicizes reality and accepts society as a natural fact. Balzac depicts the last great struggles against the capitalist degradation of man, while his successors passively register an already degraded capitalist world. This draining of direction and meaning from history results in the art we know as naturalism. By naturalism Lukács means that distortion of realism, epitomized by Zola, which merely photographically reproduces the surface phenomena of society without penetrating to their significant essences. Meticulously observed detail replaces the portrayal of 'typical' features; the dialectical relations between men and their world give way to an environment of dead, contingent objects disconnected from characters; the truly 'representative' character yields to a 'cult of the average'; psychology or physiology oust history as the true determinant of individual action. It is an alienated vision of reality, transforming the writer from an active participant in history to a clinical observer. Lacking an understanding of the typical, naturalism can create no significant totality from its materials; the unified epic or dramatic actions launched by realism collapse into a set of purely private interests.

'Formalism' reacts in an opposite direction, but betrays the same loss of historical meaning. In the alienated words of Kafka, Musil, Joyce, Beckett, Camus, man is stripped of his history and has no reality beyond the self; character is dissolved to mental states, objective reality reduced to unintelligible chaos. As with naturalism, the dialectical unity between inner and outer worlds is destroyed, and both individual and society consequently emptied of meaning. Individuals are gripped by despair and *angst*, robbed of social relations and so of authentic selfhood; history becomes pointless or cyclical, dwindled to mere duration. Objects lack significance and become merely contingent; and so symbolism gives way to allegory, which rejects the idea of immanent meaning. If naturalism is a kind of abstract objectivity, formalism is an abstract subjectivity; both diverge from that genuinely dialectical art-form (realism) whose form mediates between concrete and general, essence and existence, type and individual.

Goldmann and genetic structuralism

Georg Lukács's chief disciple, in what has been termed the 'neo-Hegelian' school of Marxist criticism, is the Rumanian critic Lucien Goldmann.[11] Goldmann is concerned to examine the structure of a literary text for the degree to which it embodies the structure of thought (or 'world vision') of the social class or group to which the writer belongs. The more closely the text approximates to a complete, coherent articulation of the social class's 'world vision', the greater is its validity as a work of art. For Goldmann, literary works are not in the first place to be seen as the creation of individuals, but of what he calls the 'trans-individual mental structures' of a social group — by which he means the structure of ideas, values and aspirations that group shares. Great writers are those exceptional individuals who manage to transpose into art the world vision of the class or group to which they belong, and to do this in a peculiarly unified and translucent (although not necessarily conscious) way.

Goldmann terms his critical method 'genetic structuralism', and it is important to understand both terms of that phrase. *Structuralism,* because he is less interested in the contents of a particular world vision than in the structure of categories it displays. Two apparently quite different writers may thus be shown to belong to the same collective mental structure. *Genetic,* because Goldmann is concerned with how such mental structures are historically produced — concerned, that is to say, with the relations between a world vision and the historical conditions which give rise to it.

Goldmann's work on Racine in *The Hidden God* is

perhaps the most exemplary model of his critical method. He discerns in Racine's drama a certain recurrent structure of categories — God, World, Man — which alter in their 'content' and interrelations from play to play, but which disclose a particular world vision. It is the world vision of men who are lost in a valueless world, accept this world as the only one there is (since God is absent), and yet continue to protest against it — to justify themselves in the name of some absolute value which is always hidden from view. The basis of this world vision Goldmann finds in the French religious movement known as Jansenism; and he explains Jansenism, in turn, as the product of a certain displaced social group in seventeenth-century France — the so-called *noblesse de robe*, the court officials who were economically dependent on the monarchy and yet becoming increasingly powerless in the face of that monarchy's growing absolutism. The contradictory situation of this group, needing the Crown but politically opposed to it, is expressed in Jansenism's refusal both of the world and of any desire to change it historically. All of this has a 'world-historical' significance: the *noblesse de robe*, themselves recruited from the bourgeois class, represent the failure of the bourgeoisie to break royal absolutism and establish the conditions for capitalist development.

What Goldmann is seeking, then, is a set of structural relations between literary text, world vision and history itself. He wants to show how the historical situation of a social group or class is transposed, by the mediation of its world vision, into the structure of a literary work. To do this it is not enough to begin with the text and work outwards to history, or vice versa; what is required is a dialectical method of criticism which moves constantly between text, world vision and history, adjusting each to the others.

Interesting as it is, Goldmann's critical enterprise seems to me marred by certain major flaws. His concept of social consciousness, for example, is Hegelian rather than Marxist: he sees it as the direct expression of a social class, just as the literary work then becomes the direct expression of this consciousness. His whole model, in other words, is too trimly symmetrical, unable to accommodate the dialectical conflicts and complexities, the unevenness and discontinuity, which characterize literature's relation to society. It declines, in his later work *Pour une Sociologie du Roman* (1964), into an essentially mechanistic version of the base-superstructure relationship.[12]

Pierre Macherey and 'decentred' form

Both Lukács and Goldmann inherit from Hegel a belief that the literary work should form a unified totality; and in this they are close to a conventional position in non-Marxist criticism. Lukács sees the work as a *constructed* totality rather than a natural organism; yet a vein of 'organistic' thinking about the art object runs through much of his criticism. It is one of the several scandalous propositions which Pierre Macherey throws out to bourgeois and neo-Hegelian criticism alike that he rejects this belief. For Macherey, a work is tied to ideology not so much by what it says as by what it does not say. It is in the significant *silences* of a text, in its gaps and absences, that the presence of ideology can be most positively felt. It is these silences which the critic must make 'speak'. The text is, as it were, ideologically forbidden to say certain things; in trying to tell the truth in his own way, for example, the author finds himself forced to reveal the limits of the ideology within which he writes. He is forced to reveal its gaps and silences, what it is unable to articulate. Because a text contains these gaps and silences, it is always *incomplete*. Far from constituting a rounded, coherent whole, it displays a conflict and contradiction of meanings; and the significance of the work lies in the difference rather than unity between these meanings. Whereas a critic like Goldmann finds in the work a central structure, the work for Macherey is always *'de-centred'*; there is no central essence to it, just a continuous conflict and disparity of meanings. 'Scattered', 'dispersed', 'diverse', 'irregular': these are the epithets which Macherey uses to express his sense of the literary work.

When Macherey argues that the work is 'incomplete', however, he does not mean that there is a piece missing which the critic could fill in. On the contrary, it is in the nature of the work to be incomplete, tied as it is to an ideology which silences it at certain points. (It is, if you like, complete in its incompleteness.) The critic's task is not to fill the work in; it is to seek out the principle of its conflict of meanings, and to show how this conflict is produced by the work's relation to ideology.

To take a fairly obvious example: in *Dombey and Son* Dickens uses a number of mutually conflicting languages — realist, melodramatic, pastoral, allegorical — in his portrayal of events; and this conflict comes to a head in the famous railway chapter, where the novel is ambiguously torn between contradictory responses to the railway (fear, protest, approval, exhilaration etc.), reflecting this in a clash of styles and symbols. The ideological basis of this ambiguity is that the novel is divided between a conventional bourgeois admiration of industrial progress and a petty-bourgeois anxiety about its inevitably disruptive effects. It sympathizes with those washed-up minor characters whom the new world has superannuated at the same time as it celebrates the progressive thrust of industrial capitalism which has made them obsolete. In discovering the principle of the work's conflict of meanings, then, we are simultaneously analysing its complex relationship to Victorian ideology.

There is, of course, a difference between conflicts in *meaning* and conflicts in *form*. Macherey attends mainly to the former; and such disparities do not necessarily result in the breakdown of unified literary form, although they are clearly closely bound up with it. In our later discussion of Walter Benjamin and Bertolt Brecht, we shall see how the Marxist argument about form is there taken a stage further, to the point where a deliberate option for 'open' rather than 'closed' forms, for conflict rather than resolution, becomes itself a political commitment.

3

The writer and commitment

Art and the proletariat

Even those only slightly acquainted with Marxist criticism know that it calls on the writer to commit his art to the cause of the proletariat. The layman's image of Marxist criticism, in other words, is almost entirely shaped by the literary events of the epoch we know as Stalinism. There was the establishment in post-revolutionary Russia of *Proletkult*, with its aim of creating a purely proletarian culture cleansed of bourgeois influences ('a laboratory of pure proletarian ideology', as its leader Bogdanov called it); the Futurist poet Mayakovsky's call for the destruction of all past art, summarized in the slogan 'burn Raphael'; the 1928 decree of the Bolshevik Party Central Committee that literature must serve the interests of the party, which sent writers out to visit construction sites and produce novels glorifying machinery. All of this comes to a head with the 1934 Congress of Soviet Writers, with its official adoption of the doctrine of 'socialist realism', cobbled together by Stalin and Gorky and promulgated by

Stalin's cultural thug Zhdanov. The doctrine taught that it was the writer's duty 'to provide a truthful, historico-concrete portrayal of reality in its revolutionary development', taking into account 'the problem of ideological transformation and the education of the workers in the spirit of socialism'. Literature must be tendentious, 'party-minded', optimistic and heroic; it should be infused with a 'revolutionary romanticism', portraying Soviet heroes and prefiguring the future.[1] The same congress heard Maxim Gorky, once a staunch defender of artistic freedom but by now a Stalinist henchman, announce that the role of the bourgeoisie in world literature had been greatly exaggerated since world culture had in fact been in decline since the Renaissance. It was also treated to Radek's paper on 'James Joyce or Socialist Realism?', which described Joyce's work as a heap of dung teeming with worms, and accused *Ulysses* (set in 1904) of historical untruthfulness since it made no reference to the Easter uprising in Ireland (1916).

There is no space here to recount in full the chilling narrative of how the loss of the Bolshevik revolution under Stalin expressed itself in one of the most devastating assaults on artistic culture ever witnessed in modern history — an assault conducted in the name of a theory and practice of social liberation.[2] A brief account will have to suffice. There was little control of artistic culture by the Bolshevik party after the 1917 revolution; until 1928, when the first five-year plan was initiated, several relatively independent cultural organizations flourished, along with a number of independent publishing houses. The relative

cultural liberalism of this period, with its medley of
artistic movements (Futurism, Formalism, Imagism,
Constructivism and so on) reflected the relative
liberalism of the so-called New Economic Policy of
those years. In 1925, the first party declaration on
literature struck a fairly neutral pose between
contending groups, refusing to commit itself to a
single trend and claiming control only in a general
way. Lunacharsky, the first Bolshevik Minister of
Culture, encouraged at this time all art forms not
openly hostile to the revolution, despite considerable
personal sympathy with the aims of *Proletkult*.
Proletkult regarded art as a class weapon and
completely rejected bourgeois culture; recognizing
that proletarian culture was weaker than its
bourgeois counterpart, it sought to develop a
distinctively proletarian art which would organize
working-class ideas and feelings towards collectivist
rather than individualist goals.

The dogmatism of *Proletkult* was continued in the
late 1920s by the All Russian Association of
Proletarian Writers (RAPP), the historical function
of which was to absorb other cultural organizations,
eliminate liberal tendencies in culture (notably
Trotsky) and prepare the path to 'socialist realism'.
Even RAPP, however, was too critical, accommoda-
ting and 'individualist' for Stalinist orthodoxy;
moreover, it had alienated 'fellow-travellers' at a
time when this ran counter to Stalin's policy. Stalin,
moving from an assertive 'proletarianism' towards a
'nationalist' ideology and alliances with 'progressive'
elements, distrusted RAPP's proletarian zeal; in
1932 it was accordingly dissolved and replaced by
the Soviet Writers Union, a direct organ of Stalin's

power of which membership was compulsory for publication. There followed throughout the 1940s and early 1950s a series of crippling literary decrees; literature itself sank to a nadir of false optimism and uniform plots. Mayakovsky had committed suicide in 1930; nine years later Vsevolod Meyerhold, the experimental theatre producer whose pioneering work influenced Brecht and was denounced as decadent, declared publicly that 'this pitiable and sterile thing called socialist realism has nothing to do with art'. He was arrested the following day and died soon afterwards; his wife was murdered.

Lenin, Trotsky and commitment

In promulgating the doctrine of socialist realism at the 1934 Congress, Zhdanov had ritually appealed to the authority of Lenin; but his appeal was in fact a distortion of Lenin's literary views. In his *Party Organisation and Party Literature* (1905), Lenin censured Plekhanov for criticizing what he consider-ed the too overtly propagandist nature of works like Gorky's *The Mother*. Lenin, in contrast, called for an openly class-partisan literature: 'Literature must become a cog and a screw of one single great social democratic machine.' Neutrality in writing, he argues, is impossible: 'the freedom of the bourgeois writer is only masked dependence on the money bag! ... Down with non-partisan writers!' What is needed is a 'broad, multiform and various litera-ture inseparably linked with the working-class movement'.

Lenin's remarks, interpreted by unsympathetic critics as applying to imaginative literature as a whole,[3] were in fact intended to apply to *party* literature. Writing at a time when the Bolshevik party was in the process of becoming a mass organization and needed strong internal discipline, Lenin had in mind not novels but party theoretical writing; he was thinking of men like Trotsky, Plekhanov and Parvus, of the need for intellectuals to adhere to a party line. His own literary interests were fairly conservative, confined on the whole to an admiration of realism; he admitted to not understanding futurist or expressionist experiments, though he considered that film was potentially the most politically important art form. In cultural affairs, however, he was generally open-minded. In his speech to the 1920 Congress of Proletarian Writers he opposed the abstract dogmatism of proletarian art, rejecting as unreal all attempts to decree a brand of culture into being. Proletarian culture could be built only in the knowledge of previous culture: all the valuable culture bequeathed by capitalism, he insisted, must be carefully preserved. 'There is no doubt', he wrote in *Concerning Art and Literature*, 'that it is literary activity which can least tolerate a mechanical egalitarianism, a domination of the minority by the majority. There is no doubt that in this domain the assurance of a rather large field of action for thought and imagination, for form and content, is absolutely essential.'[4] Writing to Gorky, he argued that an artist can glean much of value from all kinds of philosophy; the philosophy may contradict the artistic truth he communicates, but the point is what an artist creates, not what he thinks. Lenin's own articles on Tolstoy show this conviction in practice. As a spokesman for petty-bourgeois peasant interests, Tolstoy inevitably has an incorrect understanding of history since he cannot recognize that the future lies with the proletariat; but such understanding is not essential for him to produce great art. The realistic force and truthful portrayals of his fiction transcend the naive utopian ideology which frames it, revealing a contradiction between Tolstoy's art and his reactionary Christian moralism. It is, as we shall see, a contradiction of crucial relevance to Marxist criticism's attitude to the question of literary partisanship.

The second major architect of the Russian revolution, Leon Trotsky, stands with Lenin rather than with *Proletkult* and RAPP on aesthetic issues, even though Bukharin and Lunacharsky both enlisted Lenin's writings in their attack on Trotsky's cultural views. In his *Literature and Revolution*, written at a time when the majority of Russian intellectuals were hostile to the revolution and needed to be won over, Trotsky deftly combines an imaginative openness to the most fertile strains of non-Marxist post-revolutionary art with a trenchant criticism of its blindspots and limitations.[5] Opposing the Futurists' naive discarding of tradition ('We Marxists have always lived in tradition'), he insists like Lenin on the need for socialist culture to absorb the finest products of bourgeois art. The domain of culture is not one in whch the party is called to command; yet this does not mean eclectically tolerating counter-revolutionary works. A vigilant revolutionary censorship must be united with a 'broad and flexible policy in the arts'. Socialist art must be 'realist', but in no narrowly generic sense, for realism itself is intrinsically neither revolutionary nor reactionary; it is, instead, a 'philosophy of life' which should not be confined to the techniques of a particular school. 'The belief that we force poets, willy-nilly, to write about nothing but factory chimneys or a revolt against capitalism is absurd.' Trotsky, as we have seen, recognizes that artistic form is the product of social 'content', but at the same time he ascribes to it a high degree of autonomy: 'A work of art should be judged in the first place by its own law.' He thus acknowledges what is valuable in the intricate technical analyses of the Formalists, while berating them for their sterile unconcern with the social content and conditions of literary form. In its blend of principled yet flexible Marxism and perceptive practical criticism, *Literature and Revolution* is a disquieting text for non-Marxist critics. No wonder F.R. Leavis referred to its author as 'this dangerously intelligent Marxist'.[6]

Marx, Engels and commitment

The doctrine of socialist realism naturally claimed descent from Marx and Engels; but its true forbears were more properly the nineteenth-century Russian 'revolutionary democratic' critics, Belinsky, Chernyshevsky and Dobrolyubov.[7] These men saw literature as social criticism and analysis, and the artist as a social enlightener; literature should disdain elaborate aesthetic techniques and become an instrument of social development. Art reflects social reality, and must portray its typical features. The influence of these critics can be felt in the work of Georgy Plekhanov ('The Marxist Belinsky', as Trotsky called him).[8] Plekhanov censured Chernyshevsky for his propagandist demands of art, refused to put literature at the service of party politics, and distinguished rigorously between its social function and aesthetic effect; but he held that only art which serves history rather than immediate pleasure is valuable. Like the revolutionary democratic critics, too, he believes that literature 'reflects' reality. For Plekhanov, it is possible to 'translate' the language of literature into that of sociology — to find the 'social equivalent' of literary facts. The writer translates social facts into literary ones, and the critic's task is to de-code them back into reality. For Plekhanov, as for Belinsky and Lukács, the writer reflects reality most significantly by creating 'types'; he expresses 'historic individuality' in his characters, rather than depicting mere individual psychology.

Through the tradition of Belinsky and Plekhanov, then, the idea of literature as typifying and socially reflective enters into the formulation of socialist realism. 'Typicality', as we have seen, is a concept shared by Marx and Engels; yet in their own literary comments it is rarely if ever accompanied by an insistence that literary works should be politically prescriptive. Marx's own favourite authors were Aeschylus, Shakespeare and Geothe, none of them exactly revolutionary; and in an early article on the freedom of the press in the *Rheinische Zeitung* he attacks utilitarian views of literature as a means to an end. 'A writer does *not* regard his work as means to an end. They are an end in themselves; they are so little 'means' for himself and others, that he will, if necessary, sacrifice his own existence to their existence ... The first freedom of the press consists in this: that it is not a trade.' Two points need to be made here. First, Marx is speaking of the commercial rather than political uses of literature; secondly, the assertion that the press is not a trade is a piece of Marx's youthful idealism, since he clearly knew (and said) that in fact it is. But the idea that art is in some sense an end in itself crops up even in Marx's mature work: it is there in his *Theories of Surplus Value* (1905-10), where he remarks that 'Milton produced *Paradise Lost* for the same reason that a silk worm produces silk. It was an activity of *his* nature.' (In his drafts for *The Civil War in France* (1871), he compares Milton's selling his poem for five pounds with the officials of the Paris Commune, who performed public office for no great financial reward.)

Marx and Engels by no means crudely equated the aesthetically fine with the politically correct, even though political predilections naturally entered into Marx's own literary value-judgements. He liked realist, satirical, radical writers, and (apart from the folk-ballads it produced) was hostile to Romanticism, which he regarded as a poetical mystification of hard political reality. He detested Chateaubriand and saw German Romantic poetry merely as a sacred veil which concealed the sordid prose of bourgeois life, rather as Germany's feudal relations concealed it.

Marx and Engels's attitude to the question of commitment, however, is best revealed in two famous letters written by Engels to novelists who had submitted their work to him. In a letter of 1885 to

Minna Kautsky, who had sent Engels her inept and soggy recent novel, Engels wrote that he was by no means averse to fiction with a political 'tendency', but that it was wrong for an author to be *openly* partisan. The political tendency must emerge unobtrusively from the dramatized situations; only in this indirect way could revolutionary fiction work effectively on the bourgeois consciousness of its readers. 'A socialist-based novel fully achieves its purpose ... if by conscientiously describing the real mutual relations, breaking down conventional illusions about them, it shatters the optimism of the bourgeois world, instils doubt as to the eternal character of the bourgeois world, although the author does not offer any definite solution or does not even line up openly on any particular side.'

In a second letter of 1888 to Margaret Harkness, Engels criticizes her proletarian tale of the London streets (*A City Girl*) for portraying the East End masses as too inert. Picking up the novel's subtitle — 'A Realistic Story' — he comments: 'Realism to my mind implies, besides truth of detail, the truthful reproduction of typical characters under typical circumstances.' Harkness neglects true typicality because she fails to integrate into her depiction of the *actual* working class any sense of their historical role and potential development; in this sense she has produced a 'naturalist' rather than a 'realist' work.

Taken together, Engels's two letters suggest that overt political commitment in fiction is unnecessary (not, of course, unacceptable) because truly realist writing itself dramatizes the significant forces of social life, breaking beyond both the photographically observable and the imposed rhetoric of a 'political solution'. This is the concept, later to be developed by Marxist criticism, of so-called 'objective partisanship'. The author need not foist his own political views on his work because, if he reveals the real and potential forces *objectively* at work in a situation, he is already in that sense partisan. Partisanship, that is to say, is inherent in reality itself; it emerges in a method of treating social reality rather than in a subjective attitude towards it. (Under Stalinism, such 'objective partisanship' was denounced as pure 'objectivism' and replaced with a purely subjective partisanship.)

This position is characteristic of Marx and Engels's literary criticism. Independently of each other, they both criticized Lassalle's verse-drama *Franz von Sickingen* for its lack of a rich Shakespearian realism which would have prevented its characters from being mere mouthpieces of history; and they also accused Lassalle of having selected a protagonist untypical for his purposes. In *The Holy Family* (1845), Marx levels a similar criticism at Eugène Sue's best-selling novel *Les Mystères de Paris*, whose two-dimensional characters he sees as insufficiently representative.

Marx's devastating assault on Sue's moralistic melodrama also reveals another crucial aspect of his aesthetic beliefs. Marx finds the novel self-contradictory, in that what it shows diverges from what it says. The hero, for example, is meant to be morally admirable but unintentionally emerges as a self-righteous immoralist. The work is imprisoned by the French bourgeois ideology which caused it to sell so well; but at the same time it can occasionally reach beyond its ideological limits and 'deliver a slap in the face of bourgeois prejudice'. This distinction between the 'conscious' and 'unconscious' dimensions of Sue's fiction (Marx here even anticipates Freud in detecting a submerged castration complex at work in the book) is essentially one between the explicit social 'message' of the book and what, despite that, it actually discloses; and it is this distinction which enables Marx and Engels to admire a consciously reactionary author like Balzac. Despite his Catholic and legitimist prejudices, Balzac has a deeply imaginative sense of the significant movements of his own history; his novels show him forced by the power of his own artistic perceptions into sympathies at odds with his political views. He had, Marx remarks in *Capital*, 'a deep grasp of the real situation'; and Engels comments in his letter to Margaret Harkness that 'his satire is never keener, his irony never more bitter, than when he sets in motion the very men and women with whom he sympathises most deeply — the nobles'. He is a legitimist on the surface, but betrays in the depths of his fiction an undisguised admiration for his bitterest political antagonists, the republicans. It is this distinction between a work's subjective intention and objective meaning, this 'principle of contradiction', which we find re-echoed in Lenin's work on Tolstoy and Lukács's criticism of Walter Scott.[9]

The reflectionist theory

The question of partisanship in literature is bound up to some extent with the problem of how works of literature relate to the real world. Socialist realism's prescription that literature should teach certain political attitudes assumes that literature does indeed (or at least ought to) 'reflect' or 'reproduce' social reality in a fairly direct way. Marx and Engels, interestingly, do not themselves use the metaphor of 'reflection' about literary works,[10] although Marx speaks in *The Holy Family* of Eugène Sue's novel being in some respects untrue to the life of its times, and Engels could find in Homer direct illustrations of kinship systems in early Greece.[11] Nevertheless, 'reflectionism' has been a deep-seated tendency in Marxist criticism, as a way of combating formalist theories of literature which lock the literary work within its own sealed space, marooned from history.

In its cruder formulations, the idea that literature 'reflects' reality is clearly inadequate. It suggests a passive, mechanistic relationship between literature and society, as though the work, like a mirror or photographic plate, merely inertly registered what was happening 'out there'. Lenin speaks of Tolstoy as the 'mirror' of the Russian revolution of 1905; but if Tolstoy's work is a mirror, then it is, as Pierre Macherey argues, one placed at an angle to reality, a *broken* mirror which presents its images in fragmented form, and is as expressive in what it *does not* reflect as in what it does. 'If art reflects life', Bertolt Brecht comments in *A Short Organum for the Theatre* (1948), 'It does so with special mirrors'. And if we are to speak of a 'selective' mirror with certain blindspots and refractions, then it seems that the metaphor has served its limited usefulness and had better be discarded for something more helpful.

What that something is, however, is not obvious. If the cruder uses of the 'reflection' metaphor are theoretically sterile, more sophisticated versions of it are not entirely adequate either. In his essays of the 1930s and 1940s, Georg Lukács adopts Lenin's epistemological theory of reflection: all apprehension of the external world is just a reflection of it in human consciousness.[12] In other words, he accepts uncritically the curious notion that concepts are somehow 'pictures' in one's head of external reality. But true knowledge, for both Lenin and Lukács, is not thereby a matter of initial sense-impressions: it is, Lukács claims, 'a more profound and comprehensive reflection of objective reality than is given in appearance'. In other words, it is a perception of the categories which underlie those appearances — categories which are discoverable by scientific theory or (for Lukács) great art. This is clearly the most reputable form of the reflectionist theory, but it is doubtful whether it leaves much room for 'reflection'. If the mind can penetrate to the categories beneath immediate experience, then consciousness is clearly an *activity* — a *practice* which works on that experience to transform it into truth. What sense this makes of 'reflection' is then unclear. Lukàcs, indeed, wants finally to preserve the idea that consciousness is an active force: in his late work on Marxist aesthetics, he sees artistic consciousness as a creative intervention into the world rather than as a mere reflection of it.

Leon Trotsky claimed that artistic creation is 'a deflection, a changing and a transformation of reality, in accordance with the peculiar laws of art'. This excellent formulation, learnt in part from the Russian formalist theory that art involves a 'making strange' of experience, modifies any simple notion of art as reflection. Trotsky's position is taken further by Pierre Macherey. For Macherey, the effect of literature is essentially to *deform* rather than to imitate. If the image corresponds wholly to the reality (as in a mirror), it becomes identical to it and ceases to be an image at all. The baroque style of art, which assumes that the more one distances oneself from the object the more one truly imitates it, is for Macherey a model of all artistic activity; literature is essentially *parodic*.

Literature, then, one might say, does not stand in some reflective, symmetrical, one-to-one relation with its object. The object is deformed, refracted, dissolved — reproduced less in the sense that a mirror *re*produces its object than, perhaps, in the way that a dramatic performance re*produces* the dramatic text, or — if I may risk a more adventurous example — the way in which a car reproduces the materials of which it is built. A dramatic performance is clearly more than a 'reflection' of the dramatic text; on the contrary (and especially in the theatre of Bertolt Brecht), it is a transformation of the text into a unique product, which involves re-working it in accordance with the specific demands and conditions of theatrical performance. Similarly, it would be absurd to speak of a car 'reflecting' the materials which went into its making. There is no such one-to-one continuity between those materials and the finished product, because what has intervened between them is a transformative *labour*. The analogy is, of course, inexact, for what characterizes art is the fact that, in transforming its materials into a product, it reveals and distances them, which is obviously not the case with automobile production. But the comparison may stand, partial as it is, as a corrective to the case that art reproduces reality as a mirror reflects the world.

The question of how far literature is more than a mere reflection of reality brings us back to the issue of partisanship. In *The Meaning of Contemporary Realism* (1958), Lukács argues that modern writers should do more than merely reflect the despair and *ennui* of late bourgeois society; they should try to take up a critical perspective on this futility, revealing positive possibilities beyond it. To do this, they must do more than merely mirror society, for if they do so they will introduce into their art the very distortions which characterize modern bourgeois consciousness. The reflection of a distortion will become a distorted reflection. In demanding that authors should advance beyond the 'decadence' of Joyce and Beckett, however, Lukács does not ask that they should advance all the way beyond it into socialist realism. It is enough if they can manage what Soviet criticism terms 'critical realism', by which is meant that positive, critical and total conception of society characteristic of great nineteenth-century fiction and epitomized for Lukács above all by Thomas Mann. This, Lukács claims, is inferior to socialist realism, but is at least a step on the way. What Lukács is calling for, then, is essentially for the modern age to move forward into the nineteenth century. We need a return to the great tradition of critical realism; we require writers who, if not directly committed to socialism, at least 'take (socialism) into account and do not reject it out of hand'.

Lukács has been attacked on two main fronts for this position. As we shall see in the next chapter, he has been cogently criticized by Bertolt Brecht, who claims that he makes a fetish of nineteenth-century realism and is culpably blind to the best of modernist art; but he has also been upbraided by his own Communist Party comrades for his notably lukewarm attitude to socialist realism.[13] Despite some perfunctory hat-tipping to the theory of socialist realism, Lukács is in practice as critical of most of its dismal products as he is of formalist 'decadence'. Against both he posits the great humanist tradition of bourgeois realism. There is no need to share the Communist Party's defence of socialist realism to endorse their criticism of the lameness of Lukács's position — a lameness figured in that feeble plea that writers 'should at least take socialism into account'. Lukács's contrast between critical realism and formalist decadence has its roots in the cold war period when it was imperative for the Stalinist world to forge alliances with 'peace-loving' progressive bourgeois intellectuals, and so imperative to play down a revolutionary commitment. His politics at this period turn on a simplistic contrast between 'peace' and 'war' — between positive 'progressive' writers who reject *angst* and the decadent reactionaries who embrace it. Similarly, Lukács's embarrassing praise of third-rate anti-fascist authors in *The Historical Novel* reflects the politics of the Popular Front period, with its opposition of 'democracy' rather than revolutionary socialism to the growing power of fascism. Lukács, as George Lichtheim points out,[14] belongs essentially to the great classical-humanist German tradition, and regards Marxism as an extension of it; Marxism and bourgeois humanism thus form a common, enlightened front against the irrationalist tradition in Germany which culminates in fascism.

Literary commitment and English Marxism

The question of 'committed' literature has been rather less subtly argued by English Marxist criticism. It was a live issue in English Marxist criticism in the 1930s; but because of a particular theoretical confusion it remained unresolved. That confusion, first noted by Raymond Williams,[15] lies in the fact that much English Marxist criticism seems to subscribe simultaneously to a mechanistic view of art as the passive 'reflex' of the economic base, and to a Romantic belief in art as projecting an ideal world and stirring men to new values. It is a contradiction clearly marked in the work of Christopher Caudwell. Poetry for Caudwell is functional, in that it adapts men's fixed instincts to socially necessary ends by altering their feelings. The songs which accompany harvesting are a naive example: 'the instincts must be harnessed to the needs of the harvest by a social mechanism', which is art.[16] It is not difficult to see the closeness of this crudely functionalist view of art to Zhdanovism: if poetry can help on the harvest it can also speed up steel production. But Caudwell unites this view with a form of Romantic idealism more akin to Shelley than Stalin: 'Art is like a magic lantern which projects our real selves onto the Universe and promises us that we, as we desire, can alter the

Universe, alter it to the measure of our needs ...'
The shift from 'instinct' to 'desire' is interesting; art
now helps man adapt nature to himself, rather than
adapt himself to nature. In some ways this blend of
pragmatic and Romantic ideas of art resembles
Russian 'revolutionary Romanticism' — the adding
of an ideal image of what might be to a doggedly
faithful depiction of what is, in order to spur men to
higher achievements. But the confusion is com-
pounded for writers like Caudwell by the strong
influence of English Romanticism, which sees art as
embodying a world of ideal value. Caudwell
'reconciles' the two positions in the final chapter of
Illusion and Reality by speaking of poetry as a
'dream' of the future which is then a 'guide and a
spur to action'. He calls on 'fellow-travelling' poets
like Auden and Spender to abandon their bourgeois
heritage and commit themselves to the culture of the
revolutionary proletariat; but the notion that poetry
projects a 'dream' of ideal possibility is itself,
ironically, part of that bourgeois heritage. Caudwell
is finally unable to escape from this contradiction —
unable to discover any more dialectical theory of
art's relation to reality than an efficient channelling
of social energies on the one hand, and a utopian
dreaming on the other.

Other English Marxist critics of the 1930s and
1940s were equally unsuccessful in defining that
relationship. Caudwell's work influenced one of the
most valuable pieces of Marxist criticism of the
period, George Thomson's *Aeschylus and Athens*
(1941); but Thomson's pioneering study of how
Greek drama embodies changing economic and
political forms of Greek society is more impressive

than his Caudwellian thesis that the artist's role is to collect a store of social energy, creating from it a liberatory fantasy which makes men refuse to acquiesce in the world as it is. Alick West's *Crisis and Criticism* (1937) also sees art as a way of organizing 'social energy'. The value of literature is that it embodies the productive energies of society; the writer does not take the world for granted but re-creates it, revealing its true nature as a constructed product. In communicating this sense of productive energy to his readers, the writer awakens in them similar energies, rather than merely satisfying their consumer appetites. The whole argument, imaginative though it is, is notably nebulous, and the slipperiness of the unMarxist term 'energy' does not help.[17]

The notorious question which some Marxist criticism has addressed to literary works to assess their value — is its political tendency correct, does it further the cause of the proletariat? — entails the shelving of other questions about the work as 'merely' aesthetic. An instance of this dichotomy between the 'ideological' and the 'aesthetic' occurs in Lukács's *The Historical Novel*. 'It does not matter', Lukács declares, 'whether Scott or Manzoni were aesthetically superior to, say, Heinrich Mann, or at least this is not the main point. What is important is that Scott and Manzoni, Pushkin and Tolstoy, were able to grasp and portray popular life in a more profound, authentic, human and concretely historical fashion than even the most outstanding writers of our day ...' But what does 'aesthetically superior' *mean*, if not such things as 'more profound, authentic, human and concretely historical'? (I leave aside the notable vagueness of those terms.) Lukács, like several Marxist critics, is unconsciously surrendering to one *bourgeois* notion of the 'aesthetic' — the aesthetic as a mere secondary matter of style and technique.

To suggest that the question 'is the work politically progressive?' will not do as the basis of a Marxist criticism is by no means to dismiss such partisan literature as marginal. The Soviet Futurists and Constructivists who went out into the factories and collective farms, launching wall newspapers, inspecting reading rooms, introducing radio and travelling film shows, reporting to Moscow newspapers; the theatrical experimenters like Meyerhold, Erwin Piscator and Bertolt Brecht; the hundreds of 'agit-prop' groups who saw theatre as a direct intervention in the class-struggle: the enduring achievements of these men stand as a living denial of bourgeois criticism's smug assumption that art is one thing and propaganda another. Moreover, it *is* true that all major art is 'progressive', in the limited sense that any art sealed from the significant movements of its epoch, divorced from some sense of the historically central, relegates itself to minor status. What needs to be added is Marx and Engels's 'principle of contradiction': that the political views of an author may run counter to what his work objectively reveals. It should be added, too, that the question of how 'progressive' art needs to be to be valid is an *historical* question, not one to be settled dogmatically for all time. There are periods and societies where conscious, 'progressive' political commitment need not be a necessary condition for producing major art; there are other periods —

fascism, for example — when to survive and produce as an artist at all involves the kind of questioning which is likely to result in explicit commitment. In such societies, conscious political partisanship, and the capacity to produce significant art at all, go spontaneously together. Such periods, however, are not limited to fascism. There are less 'extreme' phases of bourgeois society in which art relegates itself to minor status, becomes trivial and emasculated, because the sterile ideologies it springs from yield it no nourishment — are unable to make significant connections or offer adequate discourses. In such an era, the need for explicitly revolutionary art again becomes pressing. It is a question to be seriously considered whether we are not ourselves living in such a time.

4

The author as
producer

Art as production

I have spoken so far of literature in terms of form, politics, ideology, consciousness. But all this overlooks a simple fact which is obvious to everyone, and not least to a Marxist. Literature may be an artefact, a product of social consciousness, a world vision; but it is also an *industry*. Books are not just structures of meaning, they are also commodities produced by publishers and sold on the market at a profit. Drama is not just a collection of literary texts; it is a capitalist business which employs certain men (authors, directors, actors, stagehands) to produce a commodity to be consumed by an audience at a profit. Critics are not just analysts of texts; they are also (usually) academics hired by the state to prepare students ideologically for their functions within capitalist society. Writers are not just transposers of trans-individual mental structures, they are also workers hired by publishing houses to produce commodities which will sell. 'A writer', Marx comments in   *Theories of Surplus Value*, 'is a worker not in so far as he produces ideas, but in so far as he enriches the publisher, in so far as he is working for a wage.'

It is a salutary reminder. Art may be, as Engels remarks, the most highly 'mediated' of social products in its relation to the economic base, but in another sense it is also part of that economic base — one kind of economic practice, one type of commodity production, among many. It is easy enough for critics, even Marxist critics, to forget this fact, since literature deals with human consciousness and tempts those of us who are students of it to rest content within that realm. The Marxist critics I shall discuss in this chapter are those who have grasped the fact that art is a form of social production — grasped it not as an *external* fact about it to be delegated to the sociologist of literature, but as a fact which closely determines the nature of art itself. For these critics — I have in mind mainly Walter Benjamin and Bertolt Brecht — art is first of all a social practice rather than an object to be academically dissected. We may see literature as a *text*, but we may also see it as a social activity, a form of social and economic production which exists alongside, and interrelates with, other such forms.

Walter Benjamin

This, essentially, is the approach taken by the German Marxist critic Walter Benjamin.[1] In his pioneering essay 'The Author as Producer' (1934), Benjamin notes that the question which Marxist criticism has traditionally addressed to a literary work is: What is its position with regard to the productive relations of its time? He himself, however, wants to pose an alternative question: What is the literary work's position *within* the relations of production of its time? What Benjamin means by this is that art, like any other form of production, depends upon certain techniques of production — certain modes of painting, publishing, theatrical presentation and so on. These techniques are part of the productive *forces* of art, the stage of development of artistic production; and they involve a set of social *relations* between the artistic producer and his audience. For Marxism, as we have seen, the stage of development of a mode of production involves certain social relations of production; and the stage is set for revolution when productive forces and productive relations enter into contradiction with each other. The social relations of feudalism, for example, become an obstacle to capitalism's development of the productive forces, and are burst asunder by it; the social relations of capitalism in turn impede the full development and proper distribution of the wealth of industrial society, and will be destroyed by socialism.

The originality of Benjamin's essay lies in his application of this theory to art itself. For Benjamin, the revolutionary artist should not uncritically accept the existing forces of artistic production, but should develop and revolutionize those forces. In doing so he creates new social relations between artist and audience; he overcomes the contradiction which limits artistic forces potentially available to everyone to the private property of a few. Cinema, radio, photography, musical recording: the revolutionary artist's task is to develop these new media, as well as to transform the older modes of artistic production. It is not just a question of pushing a revolutionary 'message' through existing media; it is a question of revolutionizing the media themselves. The newspaper, for example, Benjamin sees as melting down conventional separations between literary *genres*, between writer and poet, scholar and popularizer, even between author and reader (since the newspaper reader is always ready to become a writer himself). Gramophone records, similarly, have overtaken that form of production known as the concert hall and made it obsolete; and cinema and photography are profoundly altering traditional modes of perception, traditional techniques and relations of artistic production. The truly revolutionary artist, then, is never concerned with the art-object alone, but with the means of its production. 'Commitment' is more than just a matter of presenting correct political opinions in one's art; it reveals itself in how far the artist reconstructs the artistic forms at his disposal, turning authors, readers and spectators into collaborators.[2]

Benjamin takes up this theme again in his essay 'The work of Art in the Age of Mechanical Reproduction' (1933).[3] Traditional works of art, he maintains, have an 'aura' of uniqueness, privilege, distance and permanence about them; but the mechanical reproduction of, say, a painting, by replacing this uniqueness with a plurality of copies, destroys that alienating aura and allows the beholder to encounter the work in his own particular place and time. Whereas the portrait keeps its distance, the film-camera penetrates, brings its object humanly and spatially closer and so demystifies it. Film makes everyone something of an expert — anyone can take a photograph or at least lay claim to being filmed; and as such it subverts the ritual of traditional 'high art'. Whereas the traditional painting allows you restful contemplation, film is continually modifying your perceptions, constantly producing a 'shock' effect. 'Shock', indeed, is a central category in Benjamin's aesthetics. Modern urban life is characterized by the collision of fragmentary, discontinuous sensations; but whereas a 'classical' Marxist critic like Lukács would see this fact as a gloomy index of the fragmenting of human 'wholeness' under capitalism, Benjamin typically discovers in it positive possibilities, the basis of progressive artistic forms. Watching a film, moving in a city crowd, working at a machine are all 'shock' experiences which strip objects and experience of their 'aura'; and the artistic equivalent of this is the technique of 'montage'. Montage — the connecting of dissimilars to shock an audience into insight — becomes for Benjamin a major principle of artistic production in a technological age.[4]

Bertolt Brecht and 'epic' theatre

Benjamin was the close friend and first champion of Bertolt Brecht, and the partnership between the two men is one of the most absorbing chapters in the history of Marxist criticism. Brecht's experimental theatre ('epic' theatre) was for Benjamin a model of how to change not merely the political content of art, but its very productive apparatus. Brecht, as Benjamin points out, 'succeeded in altering the functional relations between stage and audience, text and producer, producer and actor'. Dismantling the traditional naturalistic theatre, with its illusion of reality, Brecht produced a new kind of drama based on a critique of the ideological assumptions of bourgeois theatre. At the hub of his critique is Brecht's famous 'alienation effect'. Bourgeois theatre, Brecht argues, is based on 'illusionism': it takes for granted the assumption that the dramatic performance should directly reproduce the world. Its aim is to draw an audience, by the power of this illusion of reality, into an empathy with the performance, to take it as real and feel enthralled by it. The audience in bourgeois theatre is the passive consumer of a finished, unchangeable art-object offered to them as 'real'. The play does not stimulate them to think constructively of *how* it is presenting its characters and events, or how they might have been different. Because the dramatic illusion is a seamless whole which conceals the fact that it is *constructed*, it prevents an audience from reflecting critically on both the mode of representation and the actions represented.

Brecht recognized that this aesthetic reflected an ideological belief that the world was fixed, given and unchangeable, and that the function of the theatre was to provide escapist entertainment for men trapped in that assumption. Against this, he posits the view that reality is a changing, discontinuous process, produced by men and so transformable by them.[5] The task of theatre is not to 'reflect' a fixed reality, but to demonstrate how character and action are historically produced, and so how they could have been, and still can be, different. The play itself, therefore, becomes a model of that process of production; it is less a reflection *of*, than a reflection *on*, social reality. Instead of appearing as a seamless whole, which suggests that its entire action is inexorably determined from the outset, the play presents itself as discontinuous, open-ended, internally contradictory, encouraging in the audience a 'complex seeing' which is alert to several conflicting possibilities at any particular point. The actors, instead of 'identifying' with their roles, are instructed to distance themselves from them, to make it clear that they are actors in a theatre rather than individuals in real life. They 'show' the characters they act (and show themselves showing them), rather than 'become' them; the Brechtian actor 'quotes' his part, communicates a critical reflection on it in the act of performance. He employs a set of gestures which convey the social relations of the character, and the historical conditions which makes him behave as he does; in speaking his lines he does not pretend ignorance of what comes next, for, in Brecht's aphorism, 'important is as important becomes'.

The play itself, far from forming an organic unity which carries an audience hypnotically through from beginning to end, is formally uneven, interrupted, discontinuous, juxtaposing its scenes in ways which disrupt conventional expectations and force the audience into critical speculation on the dialectical relations between the episodes. Organic unity is also disrupted by the use of different art-forms — film, back-projection, song, choreography — which refuse to blend smoothly with one another, cutting across the action rather than neatly integrating with it. In this way, too, the audience is constrained into a multiple awareness of several conflicting modes of representation. The result of these 'alienation effects' is, precisely, to 'alienate' the audience from the performance, to prevent it from emotionally identifying with the play in a way which paralyses its powers of critical judgement. The 'alienation effect' shows up familiar experience in an unfamiliar light, forcing the audience to question attitudes and behaviour which it has taken as 'natural'. It is the reverse of the bourgeois theatre, which 'naturalizes' the most unfamiliar events, processing them for the audience's undisturbed consumption. In so far as the audience is made to pass judgements on the performance and the actions it embodies, it becomes an expert collaborator in an open-ended practice, rather than the consumer of a finished object. The text of the play itself is always provisional: Brecht would rewrite it on the basis of the audience's reactions, and encouraged others to participate in that rewriting. The play is thus an experiment, testing its own presuppositions by feedback from the effects of performance; it is incomplete in itself, completed only in the audience's reception of it. The theatre ceases to be a breeding-ground of fantasy and comes to resemble a cross between a laboratory, circus, music hall, sports arena and public discussion hall. It is a 'scientific' theatre appropriate to a scientific age, but Brecht always placed immense emphasis on the need for an audience to enjoy itself, to respond 'with sensuousness and humour'. (He liked them to smoke, for example, since this suggested a certain ruminative relaxation.) The audience must 'think above the action', refuse to accept it uncritically, but this is not to discard *emotional* response: 'One thinks feelings and one feels thoughtfully.'[6]

Form and production

Brecht's 'epic' theatre, then, exemplifies Benjamin's theory of revolutionary art as one which transforms the modes, rather than merely the contents, of artistic production. The theory is not, in fact, wholly Benjamin's own: it was influenced by the Russian Futurists and Constructivists, just as his ideas about artistic media owed something to the Dadaists and Surrealists. It is, nonetheless, a highly significant development;[7] and I want to consider briefly three interrelated aspects of it. The first is the new meaning it gives to the idea of form; the second concerns its redefinition of the author, and the third its redefinition of the artistic product itself.

Artistic form, for long the jealously-guarded province of the aesthetes, is given a significantly new dimension by the work of Brecht and Benjamin. I have argued already that form crystallizes modes of ideological perception; but it also embodies a certain set of productive relations between artists and audiences.[8] What artistic modes of production a society has available — can it print texts by the thousand, or are manuscripts passed by hand round a courtly circle? — is a crucial factor in determining the social relations between 'producers' and 'consumers', but also in determining the very literary form of the work itself. The work which is sold on the market to anonymous thousands will characteristically differ in form from the work produced under a patronage system, just as the drama written for a popular theatre will tend to differ in formal conventions from that produced for private theatre. The relations of artistic production are in this sense *internal* to art itself, shaping its forms from within. Moreover, if changes in artistic technology alter the relations between artist and audience, they can equally transform the relations between artist and artist. We think instinctively of the work as the product of the isolated, individual author, and indeed this is how most works have been produced; but new media, or transformed traditional ones, open up fresh possibilities of collaboration *between* artists. Erwin Piscator, the experimental theatre director from whom Brecht learnt a great deal, would have a whole staff of dramatists at work on a play, and a team of historians, economists and statisticians to check their work.

The second redefinition concerns just this concept of the author. For Brecht and Benjamin, the author is primarily a *producer*, analogous to any other maker of a social product. They oppose, that is to say, the Romantic notion of the author as *creator* — as the God-like figure who mysteriously conjures his handiwork out of nothing. Such an inspirational, individualist concept of artistic production makes it impossible to conceive of the artist as a worker rooted in a particular history with particular materials at his disposal. Marx and Engels were themselves alive to this mystification of art, in their comments on Eugène Sue in *The Holy Family*: they see that to divorce the literary work from the writer as 'living historical human subject' is to 'enthuse over the *miracle-working* power of the pen'. Once the work is severed from the author's historical situation, it is bound to appear miraculous and unmotivated.

Pierre Macherey is equally hostile to the idea of the author as 'creator'. For him, too, the author is essentially a producer who works up certain given materials into a new product. The author does not make the materials with which he works: forms, values, myths, symbols, ideologies come to him already worked-upon, as the worker in a car-assembly plant fashions his product from already-processed materials. Macherey is indebted here to the work of Louis Althusser, who has provided a definition of what he means by 'practice'. 'By *practice* in general I shall mean any process of *transformation* of a determinate given raw material into a determinate *product*, a transformation effected by a determinate human labour, using determinate means (of 'production').'[9] This applies, among other things, to the practice we know as art. The artist uses certain means of production — the specialized techniques of his art — to transform the materials of language and experience into a determinate product. There is no reason why this particular transformation should be more miraculous than any other.[10]

The third redefinition in question — the nature of the art-work itself — brings us back to the problem of form. For Brecht, bourgeois theatre aimed at smoothing over contradictions and creating false harmony; and if this is true of bourgeois theatre, it is also true for Brecht of certain Marxist critics, notably George Lukács. One of the most crucial controversies in Marxist criticism is the debate between Brecht and Lukács in the 1930s over the question of realism and expressionism.[11] Lukács, as we have seen, regards the literary work as a 'spontaneous whole' which reconciles the capitalist contradictions between essence and appearance, concrete and abstract, individual and social whole. In overcoming these alienations, art recreates wholeness and harmony. Brecht, however, believes this to be a reactionary nostalgia. Art for him should expose rather than remove those contradictions, thus stimulating men to abolish them in real life; the work should not be symmetrically complete in itself, but like any social product should be completed only in the act of being used. Brecht is here following Marx's emphasis in the *Contribution to the Critique of Political Economy* that a product only fully becomes a product through consumption. 'Production', Marx argues in the *Grundrisse*, ' ... not only creates an object for the subject, but also a subject for the object.'

Realism or modernism?

Underlying this conflict is a deep-seated divergence between Brecht and Lukács on the whole question of realism — a divergence of some political importance at the time, since Lukács at this point represented political 'orthodoxy' and Brecht was suspect as a revolutionary 'leftist'. Responding to

Lukács's criticism of his art as decadently formalistic, Brecht accuses Lukács himself of producing a purely formalistic definition of realism. He makes a fetish of one historically relative literary form (nineteenth-century realist fiction) and then dogmatically demands that all other art should conform to this paradigm. In demanding this he ignores the historical basis of form: how, asks Brecht, can forms appropriate to an earlier phase of the class-struggle simply be taken over or even recreated at a later time? 'Be like Balzac — only up-to-date' is Brecht's sardonic paraphrase of Lukács's position. Lukács's 'realism' is formalist because it is academic and unhistorical, drawn from the literary realm alone rather than responsive to the changing conditions in which literature is produced. Even in literary terms its base is notably narrow, dependent on a handful of novels alone rather than on an examination of other *genres*. Lukács's case, as Brecht sees, is that of the contemplative academic critic rather than the practising artist. He is suspicious of modernist techniques, labelling them as decadent because they fail to conform to the canons of the Greeks or nineteenth-century fiction; he is a utopian idealist who wants to return to the 'good old days', whereas Brecht, like Benjamin, believed that one must start from the 'bad new days' and make something of them. *Avant-garde* forms like expressionism thus hold much of value for Brecht: they embody skills newly acquired by contemporary men, such as the capacity for the simultaneous registration and swift combination of experiences. Lukács, in contrast, conjures up a Valhalla of great 'characters' from nineteenth-century literature; but perhaps, Brecht speculates, that whole conception of 'character' belongs to a certain historical set of social relations and will not survive it. We should be searching for radically different modes of characterization: socialism forms a different kind of individual, and will demand a different form of art to realize it.

This is not to say that Brecht is abandoning the concept of realism. It is rather that he wishes to extend its scope: 'our concept of realism must be wide and political, sovereign over all conventions ... we must not derive realism as such from particular existing works, but we shall use every means, old and new, tried and untried, derived from art and derived elsewhere, to render reality to men in a form they can master.' Realism for Brecht is less a specific literary style or *genre*, 'a mere question of form', than a kind of art which discovers social laws and developments, and unmasks prevailing ideologies by adopting the standpoint of the class which offers the broadest solution to social problems. Such writing need not necessarily involve *verisimilitude*, in the narrow sense of recreating the textures and appearances of things; it is quite compatible with the widest uses of fantasy and invention. Not every work which gives us the 'real' feel of the world is in Brecht's sense realist.[12]

Consciousness and production

Brecht's position, then, is a valuable antidote to the stiff-necked Stalinist suspicion of experimental literature which disfigures a work like *The Meaning of Contemporary Realism*. The materialist aesthetics of Brecht and Benjamin imply a severe criticism of the idealist case that the work's formal integration recovers a lost harmony or prefigures a future one.[13] It is a case with a long heritage, reaching back to Hegel, Schiller and Schelling, and forwards to a critic like Herbert Marcuse.[14] The role of art, Hegel claims in the *Philosophy of Fine Art*, is to evoke and realize all the power of man's soul, to stir him into a sense of his creative plenitude. For Marx, capitalist society, with its predominance of quantity over quality, its conversion of all social products to market commodities, its philistine soullessness, is inimical to art. Consequently, art's power fully to realize human capacities is dependent on the release of those capacities by the transformation of society itself. Only after the overcoming of social alienations, he argues in the *Economic and Philosophical Manuscripts* (1844), will 'the wealth of human subjective sensuality, a musical ear, an eye for the beauty of form, in short, senses capable of human pleasures ... be partly developed ... partly engendered'.[15]

For Marx, then, the ability of art to manifest human powers is dependent on the objective movement of history itself. Art is a product of the division of labour, which at a certain stage of society results in the separation of material from intellectual work, and so brings into existence a group of artists and intellectuals relatively divorced from the material means of production. Culture is itself a kind of 'surplus value': as Leon Trotsky points out, it feeds' on the sap of economics, and a material surplus in society is essential for its growth. 'Art needs comfort, even abundance', he declares in *Literature and Revolution*. In capitalist society it is converted into a commodity and warped by ideology; yet it can still partially reach beyond those limits. It can still yield us a kind of truth — not, to be sure, a scientific or theoretical truth, but the truth of how men experience their conditions of life, and of how they protest against them.[16]

Brecht would not disagree with the neo-Hegelian critics that art reveals men's powers and possibilities; but he would want to insist that those possibilities are concrete historical ones, rather than part of some abstract, universal 'human wholeness'. He would also want to insist on the productive basis which determines how far this is possible, and in this he is at one with Marx and Engels themselves. 'Like any artist', they write in *The German Ideology* 'Raphael was conditioned by the technical advances made in art before his time, by the organisation of society, by the division of labour in the locality in which he lived ...'

There is, however, an obvious danger inherent in a concern with art's technological basis. This is the trap of 'technologism' — the belief that technical forces in themselves, rather than the place they occupy within a whole mode of production, are the determining factor in history. Brecht and Benjamin sometimes fall into this trap; their work leaves open the question of how an analysis of art as a mode of production is to be systematically combined with an analysis of it as a mode of experience. What, in other words, is the relation between 'base' and 'superstructure' *in art itself?* Theodor Adorno, Benjamin's friend and colleague, correctly criticized him for resorting on occasions to too simple a model of this relationship — for seeking out analogies or resemblances between isolated economic facts and isolated literary facts, in a way which makes the relationship between base and superstructure essentially *metaphorical*.[17] Indeed this is an aspect of Benjamin's typically idiosyncratic way of working, in contrast to the properly systematic methods of Lukács and Goldmann.

The question of how to describe this relationship within art between 'base' and 'superstructure', between art as production and art as ideological, seems to me one of the most important questions which Marxist literary criticism has now to confront. Here, perhaps, it may learn something from Marxist criticism of the other arts. I am thinking in particular about John Berger's comments on oil painting in his *Ways of Seeing* (1972). Oil painting, Berger claims, only developed as an artistic *genre* when it was needed to express a certain ideological way of seeing the world, a way of seeing for which other techniques were inadequate. Oil painting creates a certain density, lustre and solidity in what it depicts; it does to the world what capital does to social relations, reducing everything to the equality of objects. The painting itself becomes an object — a commodity to be bought and possessed; it is itself a piece of property, and represents the world in those terms. We have here, then, a whole set of factors to be interrelated. There is the stage of economic production of the society in which oil painting first grew up, as a particular technique of artistic production. There is the set of social relations between artist and audience (producer/consumer, vendor/purchaser) with which that technique is bound up. there is the relation between those artistic property-relations, and property-relations in general. And there is the question of how the ideology which underpins those property-relations embodies itself in a certain form of painting, a certain way of seeing and depicting objects. It is this kind of argument, which connects modes of production to a facial expression captured on canvas, which Marxist literary criticism must develop in its own terms.

There are two important reasons why it must do so. First, because unless we can relate past literature, however indirectly, to the struggle of men and women against exploitation, we shall not fully understand our own present and so will be less able to change it effectively. Secondly, because we shall be less able to *read* texts, or to produce those art forms which might make for a better art and a better society. Marxist criticism is not just an alternative technique for interpreting *Paradise Lost* or *Middlemarch*. It is part of our liberation from oppression, and that is why it is worth discussing at book length.

Notes

Chapter 1

1 See M. Lifshitz, *The Philosophy of Art of Karl Marx* (London, 1973). For a naively prejudiced but reasonably informative account of Marx and Engels's literary interests, see P. Demetz, *Marx, Engels and the Poets* (Chicago,1967).

2 See Karl Marx and Frederick Engels, *On Literature and Art* (New York, 1973), for a compendium of these comments.

3 See especially L. Shücking, *The Sociology of Literary Taste* (London, 1944); R. Escarpit, *The Sociology of Literature* (London, 1971); R.D. Altick, *The English Common Reader* (Chicago, 1957); and R. Williams, *The Long Revolution* (London, 1961). Representative recent works have been D. Laurenson and A. Swingewood, *The Sociology of Literature* (London, 1972) and M. Bradbury, *The Social Context of English Literature* (Oxford, 1971). For an account of Raymond Williams important work, see my article in *New Left Review* 95 (January-February, 1976).

4 Much non-Marxist criticism would reject a term like 'explanation', feeling that it violates the 'mystery' of literature. I use it here because I agree with Pierre Macherey, in his *Pour Une Théorie de la Production Littéraire* (Paris, 1966), that the task of the critic is not to 'interpret' but to 'explain'. For Macherey, 'interpretation' of a text means revising or correcting it in accordance with some ideal norm of what it should be; it consists, that is to say, in refusing the text *as it is*. Interpretative criticism merely 'redoubles' the text, modifying and

elaborating it for easier consumption. In saying *more* about the work, it succeeds in saying *less*.

5 See especially Vico's *The New Science* (1725); Madame de Staël, *Of Literature and Social Institutions* (1800); H. Taine, *History of English Literature* (1863).

6 This, inevitably, is a considerably over-simplified account. For a full analysis, see N. Poulantzas, *Political Power and Social Classes* (London, 1973).

7 Quoted in the preface to Henri Arvon's *Marxist Aesthetics* (Cornell, 1970).

8 On the question of how a writer's personal history interlocks with the history of his time, see J.-P. Sartre, *The Search for a Method* (London, 1963).

9 Introduction to the *Grundrisse* (Harmondsworth, 1973).

10 See Stanley Mitchell's essay on Marx in Hall and Walton (ed.), *Situating Marx* (London, 1972).

11 Appendices to the 'Short Organum on the Theatre', in J. Willett (ed.), *Brecht on Theatre: The Development of an Aesthetic* (London, 1964).

12 To put the issue in more complex theoretical terms: the influence of the economic 'base' on *The Waste Land* is evident not in a direct way, but in the fact that it is the economic base which in the last instance determines the state of development of each element of the superstructure (religious, philosophical and so on) which went into its making, and moreover determines the structural inter-relations between those elements, of which the poem is a particular conjuncture.

13 In his 'Letter on Art in reply to André Daspre', in *Lenin and Philosophy* (London, 1971). See also the following essay on the abstract painter Cremonini.

14 Reprinted as *Articles on Tolstoy* (Moscow, 1971).

Chapter 2

1 See, for example, Ernst Fischer in his *The Necessity of Art* (Harmondsworth, 1963).

2 See my 'Marxism and Form' in C.B. Cox and Michael Schmidt (eds.), *Poetry Nation No. 1* (Manchester, 1973).

3 For a valuable account of Russian Formalism, see V. Erlich,

Russian Formalism: History and Doctrine (The Hague, 1955).

4 See Caudwell's remarks on poetry in *Illusion and Reality* (London, 1937), and his *Romance and Realism* (Princeton, 1970); see also Francis Mulhern's article on Caudwell's aesthetics in *New Left Review*, no. 85 (May/June, 1974). I do not intend to imply that Caudwell, who heroically attempted to construct a total Marxist aesthetics in notably unpropitious conditions, is merely dismissable as 'vulgar Marxist'.

5 *The Rise of the Novel* (London, 1947).

6 Reprinted in his *Art and Social Life* (London, 1953).

7 *Drama from Ibsen to Brecht* (London, 1968).

8 See R. Barthes, *Writing Degree Zero* (London, 1967).

9 Lukács was born in Budapest in 1885, the son of a wealthy banker, and in his early intellectual development came under a number of influences including that of Hegel. Two early works were *The Soul and Its Forms* (1911), and *The Theory of the Novel* (1920). He joined the Communist party in 1918 and became commissar for education in the short-lived Hungarian Soviet Republic, escaping to Austria when it fell. In 1923 he produced his major theoretical work, *History and Class Consciousness*, which was condemned as idealist by the Comintern. When Hitler came to power he emigrated to Moscow, devoting his time to literary studies; from this period date *Studies in European Realism* (London, 1972) and *The Historical Novel* (London, 1962). In 1945 he returned to Hungary, and in 1956 became Minister of Culture in Nagy's government after the anti-Russian uprising. He was deported for a year to Rumania, but later allowed to return. He also published *The Meaning of Contemporary Realism* (London, 1963), and works on Lenin, Hegel, Goethe and aesthetics.

10 In an article in the *New Hungarian Quarterly*, vol.xiii, no. 47 (Autumn 1972).

11 See in particular *The Hidden God* (London, 1964); *Towards a Sociology of the Novel* (London, 1975); *The Human Sciences and Philosophy* (London, 1966). Important articles by Goldmann available in English are: 'Criticism and Dogmatism in Literature', in D. Cooper (ed.), *The Dialectics of Liberation* (Harmondsworth, 1968); 'The

Sociology of Literature: Status and Problems of Method', in *International Social Science Journal*, vol.xix, no. 4 (1967); and 'Ideology and Writing', *Times Literary Supplement*, September 28, 1967. See also Miriam Glucksmann, 'A Hard Look at Lucien Goldmann', *New Left Review* no.56 (July/ August, 1969), and Raymond Williams, 'From Leavis to Goldmann', *New Left Review* no.67 (May/June, 1971).

12 See Adrian Mellor, 'The Hidden Method: Lucien Goldmann and the Sociology of Literature', in Birmingham University *Working Papers in Cultural Studies* no.4 (Spring, 1973). It is worth mentioning briefly here a few of the other limitations of Goldmann's work. These seem to me: an incorrect contrast between 'world vision' and 'ideology'; an elusiveness about the problem of aesthetic value; an unhistorical conception of 'mental structures'; and a certain positivistic strain in some of his working methods.

Chapter 3

1 See A.A. Zhdanov, *On Literature, Music and Philosophy* (London, 1950). Zhdanov does however allow writers to use pre-revolutionary *forms* to express their post-revolutionary content.

2 Useful accounts can be found in M. Hayward and L. Labetz (eds.), *Literature and Revolution in Soviet Russia 1917-62* (London, 1963), and R.A. Maguire, *Red Virgin Soil: Soviet Literature in the 1920s* (Princeton, 1968).

3 George Steiner, for example, in 'Marxism and Literature', *Language and Silence* (London, 1967).

4 Quoted by Henri Arvon, op.cit.

5 See Isaac Deutscher, *The Prophet Unarmed* (London, 1959) ch. 3, for a more general discussion of Trotsky's cultural attitudes and activities.

6 In 'Under Which King, Bezonian?', *Scrutiny* vol.1, 1932.

7 See Lukács's essay on them in *Studies in European Realism*, and H.E. Bowman, *Vissarian Belinsky* (Harvard, 1954).

8 See his *Letters Without Address* and *Art and Social Life* (London, 1953).

9 Lenin had not in fact read Engels's comments on Balzac when he wrote his Tolstoy articles.

10 I am indebted for this point to Professor S.S. Prawer of Oxford University.
11 In *The Origin of the Family, Private Property and the State* (1884).
12 See *Writer and Critic* (London, 1970). Lenin's theory is to be found in his *Materialism and Empirio-Criticism* (1909).
13 See Cultural Theory Panel attached to the Central Committee of the Hungarian Socialist Workers Party, 'Of Socialist Realism', in L. Baxandall (ed.), *Radical Perspectives in the Arts* (Harmondsworth, 1972).
14 *Lukács* (London, 1970).
15 In *Culture and Society 1780-1950* (London, 1958), part 3, ch. 5: 'Marxism and Culture'.
16 See *Illusion and Reality* (London, 1937).
17 West's argument is oddly similar to Jean-Paul Sartre's in *What Is Literature?* (London, 1967). Sartre argues there that the reader responds to the *created* character of writing, and so to the writer's freedom; conversely, the writer appeals to the reader's freedom to collaborate in the production of his work. The act of writing aims at a total renewal of the world; the goal of art is to 'recover' an inert world by giving it as it is but as if it had its source in human freedom. Sartre's remarks on 'commitment' in writing, though in a similarly individualist, existentialist vein, are also relevant. See also David Caute, *The Illusion* (London, 1971), ch. 1: 'On Commitment'.

Chapter 4

1 Benjamin was born in Berlin in 1892, the son of a wealthy Jewish family. As a student he was active in radical literary movements, and wrote a doctoral thesis on the origins of German baroque tragedy, later published as one of his important works. He worked as a critic, essayist and translator in Berlin and Frankfurt after the first world war, and was introduced to Marxism by Ernst Bloch; he also became a close friend of Bertolt Brecht. He fled to Paris in 1933 when the Nazis came to power and lived there until 1940, working on a study of Paris which became known as the Arcades Project. After the fall of France to the Nazis he was

caught trying to escape to Spain, and committed suicide.

2   'The Author as Producer' can be found in Benjamin's *Understanding Brecht* (London, 1973). Cf. The Italian Marxist Antonio Gramsci: 'The mode of being of the new intellectual can no longer consist in eloquence, which is an exterior and momentary mover of passions and feelings, but in active participation in practical life, as constructor, organizer, "permanent persuader" and not just a simple orater ...': *Prison Notebooks* (London, 1971).

3   Reprinted in W. Benjamin, *Illuminations* (London, 1970).

4   For the 'shock' effect, see Benjamin's *Charles Baudelaire: Lyric Poet in the Age of High Capitalism* (London, 1973). See also his essay in *Illuminations* on 'Unpacking My Library', where he considers his own passion for collecting. For Benjamin, collecting objects, far from being a way of harmoniously ordering them into a sequence, is an acceptance of the chaos of the past, of the uniqueness of the collected objects, which he refuses to reduce to categories. Collecting is a way of destroying the oppressive authority of the past, redeeming fragments from it.

5   I leave aside the question of how far Brecht, in holding this view, is guilty of a 'humanist' revision of Marxism.

6   See *Brecht on Theatre: the Development of an Aesthetic*, translated by John Willett (London, 1964), for a collection of some of Brecht's most important aesthetic writings. See also his *Messingkauf Dialogues* (London, 1965); Walter Benjamin, *Understanding Brecht*; D. Suvin, 'The Mirror and the Dynamo', in L. Baxandall, op.cit; and Martin Esslin: *Brecht: A Choice of Evils* (London, 1959). Most of Brecht's major drama is available in the two-volume Methuen edition (London, 1960-62).

7   Its implications for modern media have been discussed by Hans Magnus Enzensberger in 'Constituents of a Theory of the Media', *New Left Review* no.64 (November/December, 1970).

8   See Alf Louvre, 'Notes on a Theory of Genre', *Working Papers in Cultural Studies* no.4 (University of Birmingham, Spring, 1973).

9   *For Marx* (English edition, London, 1969). Cf. Althusser's comment in *Lenin and Philosophy*: 'The aesthetics of con-

sumption and the aesthetics of creation are merely one and the same.'

10 Macherey is in fact opposed in the final analysis to the whole idea of the author as 'individual subject', whether 'creator' or 'producer', and wants to displace him from his privileged position. It is not so much that the author produces his text as that the text 'produces itself' through the author. Parallel notions have been developed by the group of Marxist semioticians gathered around the Parisian journal *Tel Quel*, who see the literary text as a constant 'productivity' with the aid of insights derived from Marxism and Freudianism.

11 See Bertolt Brecht, 'Against George Lukács', *New Left Review* no.84 (March/April, 1974), and H. Arvon, op.cit. See also Helga Gallas, 'George Lukács and the League of Revolutionary Proletarian Writers', *Working Papers in Cultural Studies* no.4.

12 Brecht's position here should be distinguished from that of the French Marxist Roger Garaudy in his *D'un réalisme sans rivages* (Paris, 1963). Garaudy also wants to extend the term 'realism' to authors previously excluded from it; but like Lukács and unlike Brecht he still identifies aesthetic value with the great realist tradition. It is just that he is more liberal about its boundaries than Lukács.

13 See S. Mitchell, 'Lukács's Concept of The Beautiful', in G.H.R. Parkinson (ed.), *George Lukács: The Man, His Work, His Ideas* (London, 1970), for an account of Lukác's aesthetic views.

14 See in particular his *Negations* (London, 1968), *An Essay on Liberation* (London, 1969), and his essay 'Art as Form of Reality', *New Left Review* no.74 (July/August, 1972).

15 See I. Mezaros's comments on Marxist aesthetics in *Marx's Theory of Alienation* (London, 1970).

16 Though art is not in itself a scientific mode of truth, it can, nevertheless, communicate the *experience* of such a scientific (i.e., revolutionary) understanding of society. This is the experience which *revolutionary* art can yield us.

17 See Adorno on Brecht, *New Left Review* no. 81 (September/October, 1973).

Select bibliography

A comprehensive bibliography of Marxist literary cricism is to be found in Lee Baxandall's *Marxism and Aesthetics* (New York, 1968). The references to Marxist critical works in the text and footnotes of this book provide a reasonable wide-ranging reading list on the subject; but I have selected below some of the more important texts, and their most easily available editions.

L. Althusser, *Lenin and Philosophy* (London, 1971). A collection of Althusser's articles on Marxist theory, including his significant discussion of the relations between art and ideology ('Letter to André Daspre').

H. Arvon, *Marxist Aesthetics* (Ithaca, N.Y., 1970). A brief, lucid, general survey of the field, with an important account of the Brecht-Lukács controversy.

W. Benjamin, *Understanding Brecht* (London, 1973). A collection of Benjamin's journalistic writing on Brecht, incorporating theoretically crucial work like the essay on 'The Author as Producer', as well as more fragmentary and eclectic material.

B. Brecht, *On Theatre* (ed. J. Willett, London, 1973). A valuable selection of Brecht's comments on the theoretical and practical aspects of dramatic production, with useful editorial annotations.

C. Caudwell, *Illusion and Reality* (London, 1973). The major theoretical work of Marxist criticism to emerge from England in the 1930s, crude and slipshod in many of its formulations, but intent on producing a total theory of the nature of art and the development of English literature from its early beginnings to the twentieth century.

P. Demetz, *Marx, Engels and the Poets* (Chicago, 1967). A detailed though naively biased account of Marx and Engels as literary critics, with chapters on the subsequent development of Marxist criticism.

E. Fisher, *The Necessity of Art* (Harmondsworth, 1963). An ambitious though sometimes crude and reductive account of the historical origins of art, its relations with ideology and a number of other topics central to Marxist criticism.

L. Goldmann, *The Hidden God* (London, 1964). Goldmann's major critical work: a Marxist study of Pascal and Racine, with an important preliminary account of his 'genetic structuralist' method.

F. Jameson, *Marxism and Form* (Princeton, 1971). A difficult but valuable meditation on some major Marxist critics (Adorno, Benjamin, Marcuse, Bloch, Lukács, Sartre), with a suggestive final chapter on the meaning of a 'dialectical' criticism.

V.I. Lenin, *Articles on Tolstoy* (Moscow, 1971). A collection of Lenin's articles on Tolstoy as the 'mirror of the Russian revolution'.

M. Lifshitz, *The Philosophy of Art of Karl Marx* (London, 1973). A powerful and original study which analyses the relations between Marx's aesthetic views and his general theory, incorporating aspects of his aesthetic writings little known in England.

G. Lukács, *Studies in European Realism* (London, 1972); *The Historical Novel* (London, 1962). Two of Lukács's major works, in which almost all of his central critical concepts are developed. *The Meaning of Contemporary Realism* (London, 1969). A record of Lukács's attempt to come to terms with 'modernist' writing: Kafka, Musil, Joyce, Beckett and others. *Writer and Critic* (London, 1970). An uneven collection of some of Lukács's critical articles, including an important defence of the 'reflectionist' concept of art.

P. Macherey, *Pour Une Théorie de la Production Littéraire* (Paris, 1970). A challenging and original application of the Marxist theory of Louis Althusser to literary criticism, genuinely innovating in its break with 'neo-Hegelian' Marxist criticism.

Marx and Engels, *On Literature and Art* ed. L. Baxandall and S. Morawski (New York, 1973). A full compendium of Marx and Engels's scattered comments on the subject.

G. Plekhanov, *Art and Social Life* (London, 1953). A collection of Plekhanov's major essays on literature.

J.-P. Sartre, *What is Literature?* (London, 1967). A hybrid of Marxism and existentialism which contains suggestive comments about the writer's relation to language and political commitment.

L. Trotsky, *Literature and Revolution* (Ann Arbor, 1971). A classic of Marxist criticism, recording the confrontation between Marxist and non-Marxist schools of criticism in Bolshevik Russia.

Index